WHO'S HOOVER?

WHO'S HOOVER?

By
WILLIAM HARD
Author of "THE WOMEN OF TOMORROW"
Co-author of "RAYMOND ROBINS' OWN STORY OF
BOLSHEVIK RUSSIA"

DODD, MEAD AND COMPANY
NEW YORK - - - 1928

PRINTED IN THE U. S. A. BY
Quinn & Boden Company, Inc.
BOOK MANUFACTURERS
RAHWAY   NEW JERSEY

ACKNOWLEDGMENT

In the preparation of this book the author has made use of some occasional material already gathered by him for articles in the *Review of Reviews* and *Good Housekeeping*.

VIEWPOINT

PANEGYRIC is not the purpose of this book. Every four years we have enough campaign toffy—and too much.

What is a great man? He is great only by a margin. Often the margin is very narrow.

This is especially so in these times of intensive clash of efforts and enormous disparity of rewards. To-day, more than ever, a millimeter of difference in ability may mean a mile of difference in fortune and in fame.

I shall, therefore, not assume that the mile which separates Mr. Hoover in the world's eye from what we call "the ordinary man" is an exact measure of his greatness. It may be a much exaggerated measure. We need no longer be dazzled by celebrity. It is becoming commonplace. Let us look, rather, at that marginal difference of character and of brain and of luck that has occasioned the celebrity.

This book accordingly is dedicated less to Mr. Hoover's achievements than to his characteristics, less to his conquests than to his qualities, less to his glory than to his nature.

In particular it is dedicated to that part of his nature which in association with his long and wide experience of men and of affairs may be thought to fit him—or unfit him—for public political life.

To me it is of relatively small moment that Mr. Hoover and his engineering associates were able to recover a million or so of tons of zinc from the "tailings"—or refuse-dumps—of an old mine at Broken Hill in Australia by means of an ingenious use of the "flotation process." I see little connection between such accomplishments and worthiness to hold public political office.

Mr. Hoover has set himself up among us to be a public man. Scientific knowledge and engineering skill are as likely to be handicaps as they are likely to be helps to a public man. They turn the mind toward exactness. Politics is not exact. It is fluid, discursive, capricious, psychological, intuitive.

Politics is a playing upon all the keys of the whole piano of human instincts, prepossessions, prejudices, ignorances, loyalties, ambitions, aspirations, material bonds, spiritual hopes.

Mr. Hoover is far from being an old man. He is far indeed from being a man who will readily relinquish any design to which he has set himself. He will be publicly active among us for many years to come.

The basic question about him is:

Has he the political pianist's touch?

It is in an approach to the answer to that question that the experiences of his life are in this book reviewed.

CONTENTS

CHAPTER ONE

QUAKER YOUTH

In the Spring of 1893, in the student-body of Leland Stanford, Jr., University, at Palo Alto in California, there was an election-contest of enormous intensity. It seemed to those who participated in it to be also of enormous significance—and novelty. Its significance really was that it contained no novelty at all.

The ancient battle between "class" and "mass" was simply to be fought out all over again. The "class" in this instance consisted of those crusted patricians who held membership in Greek-letter fraternities. The "mass" consisted of those grubbing plebeians for whom the portals of the fraternities had never swung open.

Many of these latter creatures lived abjectly in wooden shacks once used by the workmen who had toiled to construct the University buildings. In those shacks—collectively called "The Camp"—they ate food which they themselves had cooked.

Little time had they to learn dancing, in addition to cooking, and to commend themselves

1

to the notice of feminine festive eyes and to become "queeners." This social delinquency on their part intensified their degradation as non-Greeks, as "barbarians."

The student-body offices had belonged, as of right, to the Greeks, to the fraternity aristocrats. On the fresh shores of the Pacific Ocean there was being reënacted, in childish miniature, all the wrong and all the revolt of early Athens, of young Rome.

Did the patricians, did the Coriolani and the Mamilii and the Papilii, insist always upon having the consuls? Well, then, sir! There will be Bruti and Gracchi! There will be Tribunes of the People!

The first Tribune of the People in the student-body of Leland Stanford was a boy called "Sosh." This was derisively short for "Socialist." Thus do the people's enemies always pour out persiflage upon the people's champions! The young proletarian leader's splendid real name, replete with promise, was Zion.

Zion set himself up to rally the disinherited toward vengeance—and office.

Leland Stanford had not then yet completed the second year of its academic existence. United States Senator Stanford, its founder and endower, had expressly dedicated it to the task of "making men and women useful." It lay on the westernmost frontier of the world's westernmost frontier country. Yet within less than eighteen months it had achieved the maturity of a division and a rupture between the immemorial factions of wealth and of commonwealth.

Zion had needed an emissary to carry the message of emancipation to the most "barbarous" of the "barbarians"—those who lived in "The Camp."

He had found him in a boy who seemed more boyish, more immature, shyer, than almost anybody else in the student-body. This boy seldom spoke. When he did speak, he seldom persisted beyond his first few words. He delivered newspapers to other boys. He collected and returned other boys' packages of laundry. He served as a sort of secretary-clerk to the Professor of Geology. He tapped rocks. He kept accounts in which he entered expenditures of pennies. He had a laugh which was only a chuckle. He choked this chuckle before the sound of it could become an obvious noise. On Zion's behalf, on behalf of the Tribune who aspired now actually to being Consul, to being President of the Student-Body, this dumb lad went to "The Camp" and burst into speech.

He came from Salem, Oregon. His name was Herbert Hoover.

He had worked as office-boy in the real-estate business of his uncle, John Minthorn, in Salem. He previously had worked as chore-boy and as errand-boy and, in general, as handy-boy in Newberg, Oregon, in the purlieus of the Pacific Academy which his uncle had been engaged in establishing.

Up to the time of his fifteenth or sixteenth birthday he had done little or nothing of even potential note. His biographers have been hard put to it to adorn his boyhood with purple passages indicative of his imperial future. They have been reduced—for the most part— to describing him dropping downwards on a hill on a sled or rising upwards on a tree with the help of his knees and his hands in a manner undistinguishable from the ordinary operations of gravity or from the universal juvenile impulsion toward peeping over the rims of nests of birds at eggs.

The true point in Hoover's boyhood is not any remarkable outbreak by him from his environment. It is the commonplace fidelity with which he became—and was—and is—the product of that environment. His boyhood is interesting only because—but precisely because— it explains the fundamentals, the irremovable fundamentals, of his present character.

It was natural that he was working in Stanford and that he had worked in Salem and in Newberg.

He had always worked. He came of pioneer stock which did not tolerate idle children. He came of Quaker stock for whom idleness was not only waste but sin.

His father's people had pioneered from Maryland to North Carolina before the Revolution. They had pioneered from North Carolina to Ohio before the War of 1812. They had pioneered from Ohio to Iowa before the Civil War. Hoover's uncle, John Minthorn, had now reached the Pacific Slope.

In each instance the remove was not merely to a new region. In each instance it was to the actual fresh creating of a new settlement, a new community, a new focus of human habitation, which had not previously existed.

The focus in each case was a Quaker meeting-house. The migration to North Carolina produced a new meeting-house and a new village in Randolph County on the edge of the Blue and Smoky mountain-barriers beyond which lay the trails to Tennessee and to Kentucky and to our First West. The migration to Ohio produced a new meeting-house and a new village in Miami County on the edge of what is now the Indiana line. The migration to Iowa produced a new meeting-house and a new village in Cedar

County not very far from the spot where the
Cedar River mingles with the Mississippi. The
migration to Oregon produced a new meeting-
house and a new village in Yamhill County not
very far from the waters of the Western Ocean.

It was almost by ancestral momentum that
Herbert Hoover, upon being graduated from
Leland Stanford, was to seek his fortune still
westward, across the Pacific, in Australia, in
China, in India.

He could carry with him, however, on that
far journey no local background except that of
America, no religious background except that
of Quakerism. The recollections of the Hoover
family did not extend back of Maryland. They
did not reach Europe. They did not extend
back of the Quaker faith. They did not reach
the old established churches from which the
Quakers had separated themselves.

The Hoovers in racial and national consciousness were wholly American, wholly new.
In religious consciousness they were wholly
Quaker, wholly new. The old countries of
Europe, the old creeds of the Middle Ages and
even of the Early Protestant Lutheran and Cal-
vinistic Reformation, did not remain at all in
their memories or in their mental manners.
The most ancient start of their conscious psy-

chology was Andrew Hoover, of Maryland, colonist, Quaker.

In the offspring of such a line one will search in vain for any sensitiveness to those tender ties which unite so many Americans in known and felt kinship to this or that country of the Old World. Presumably the Hoovers, being Quakers, had at one time or another become assimilated to the English stock. On the other hand, the name Hoover or Huber or Hoefer is a current commonplace name in Central and Northwestern Continental Europe. A Max Huber of Switzerland now sits as a judge at The Hague in the Permanent Court of International Justice; and the Andrew Hoover from whom in America Herbert Hoover is derived may well have been distantly linked by family blood to that Andreas Hoefer, of the Austrian Tyrol, whose immortal military exploits were brought to their earthly end only by the immortal meanness of Napoleon and the shots of a firing-squad in the breast of a disarmed defenseless prisoner-of-war.

The Continent, however, equally with England, was almost as Nineveh or Tyre to the Hoovers in their knowledge only of the New World about them. They transmitted to Herbert Hoover a page of thought on which, after

he had written "America," and after he had
written "Quaker," he could write whatever
those first two words would permit.

The first additional word that he wrote was
in truth a word beyond his control. It was dictated by the words already inscribed upon the
page. It was the word work.

His parents caused him to work in West
Branch, Iowa, in and about their cottage (in
which he was born), and in and about their
shop, in which there was a blacksmith's forge
and an agency for the sale of agricultural implements; and then, before he had completed his
tenth year, his parents both were dead.

From that time forward his life for many
years was a steady deepening of his natural
shyness and balkiness in combat with the hal-
ters and traces of ever new environments.
Thrust from the home of his birth in West
Branch in 1884, he was to have no really abiding day-after-day and year-after-year home,
untorn by travels, till he entered into the immediate service of the Federal Government in
the District of Columbia in 1917. Between
West Branch, Iowa, and Washington, D. C., he
did thirty-three years of incessant wandering.

In the Quaker conception of existence, as applied to young Herbert Hoover in 1884, there
was just one instant career for an orphan. It

was friendly care by relatives and by members of the meeting,—and prayerfully intensified labor by the orphan.

Quakers believe with a divided but equal fervor in helpfulness and self-help. An observant intimate of the adult Hoover in San Francisco once said:

"Put on old clothes and stop Herbert Hoover on the street and ask him for a dime. You will be unlikely to get it. You will be likely, on the contrary, to find yourself giving him something: namely, your name and address. You will then be likely, further, to get a visit from an agency which will strive to induce you to go to work. Only if there is no work to be got for you, or only if you are physically or mentally unable to take it, will you find that Hoover has given the agency a fund to be freely spent upon cases such as yours."

Hoover's own childhood case was handled upon that same Quaker principle of hard-headedness as the tandem-horse to soft-heartedness. It was handled on the principle laid down at Balby in England, in 1656, in the first general code of rules—for the governance of the spiritual life—drafted by approved "Elders" from among those who by the world were called Quakers but who called themselves Friends and who also called themselves Children of Light.

Rule Twelve of that code was:

"The needs of widows and of the fatherless are to be supplied. Such as can work, and do not, are to be admonished. If they refuse to work, neither let them eat. The children of needy parents are to be put to honest employment."

It is often said now that Herbert Hoover, in his humanitarianism, should be more human. He should be more personal. To put it *ad absurdum,* he should cry more when he holds the bottle to the lips of a starving Czechoslovak baby or when he hauls a dripping Mississippian out of the waves of the whelming flood.

There is some justice in this criticism. Herbert Hoover can do things more intensely personal with a more helpless and hopeless impersonality than almost anybody else.

A cabinet colleague of his not long ago suffered a grievous domestic bereavement. Hoover went to see him the next day and said nothing at all about the bereavement. He only said, as he was leaving, after much silence:

"Come to my house and stay for a while. Nobody will bother you there."

Part of the reason for this verbal impersonality of his toward others is to be found in his insistent silent demand that others shall exhibit it toward him. He hates and resents all intrusions of curiosity upon his purely personal characteristics or his purely personal feelings.

Any casual interviewer can make him blush and stammer by inquiries directed toward an exact statement of the color of his eyes. He once was tempted even toward repressive measures against a certain book about himself because, among other similar intimacies of narration, it recounted a few extremely moderately sentimental remarks alleged to have been addressed by him to the young lady whom he subsequently married.

A succeeding book which managed to avoid outraging his ingrowing passion for personal privacy contains the following description of the consequences of his first meeting with that young lady—in the geological laboratory of Leland Stanford:

"Hoover and Miss Henry fell into conversation about the carboniferous period."

The depth of that approach to the gayeties and sanctities of courtship would be the deepest depth that a reporter would ever reach in any talk with Hoover himself about it.

He is in this general matter a replica of Robert Browning. Browning has a poem called "House" which begins:

"Shall I sonnet-sing you about myself?"

It then suggests that a man seeking fame might open his private apartments to the public for their view; but it instantly indignantly exclaims:

" 'For a ticket, apply to the Publisher?'
"No! Thanking the public, I must decline.
"A peep through my window, if folks prefer!
"But, please you, no foot over threshold of
        mine!' "

Hoover is delighted to have people talk about his external achievements in the study of the carboniferous period, and in the development of the Kyshtym copper property in Russia, and in the rescue of Louisiana parishes from the destructiveness of loose water; but he flinches in almost physical pain from any probe—even the friendliest, even the most sympathetic— reaching toward Herbert Hoover the man, the brother, the husband, the father.

Guarding then his own threshold so impersonally, he equally impersonally stops short of the thresholds of others. This becomes most particularly so if he has conferred upon them any benefits. It is enough, he seems to think, that they should have to bear those benefits. Why should they have to bear also him?

That is probably the first part of the reason

for his recoil from personalism in his philanthropy. The second part rests on the tenets of the Quaker meeting-house and on the practices of every Quaker social unit.

Philanthropy among Quakers is not an emotional favor. It is an automatic duty. Its purpose is not merit by the giver and gratitude by the receiver. Its purpose is the restoration of the community to economic health. Few Quaker communities have ever existed that did not succeed in maintaining a robust (even if sometimes a rude and rough) economic health and happiness. Individual philanthropy is in such communities only a silent means to a social end.

Hoover, by breeding, takes that same view of his humanitarian endeavors in Belgium, in Central Europe, in Eastern Europe, in the Mississippi Valley. He thinks less of the loving-kindness of the means than of the ultimate, hard, practical, self-supporting, self-respecting upstandingness of the end.

Here are people laid low. What is the point? The point is not the bending over them. Any Christian will do that! That needs simply sensibility. The point is to get them to walking on their own feet. That needs sense.

Your perfected Quaker is an egg dropped in the milk of human charity, but boiled ten minutes. He is preoccupied not with reactions but with results. He is capable of considerable righteous ruthlessness.

In the course of the political campaign of 1924, at Los Angeles, California, Hoover made a radio speech in which he said:

"In America we want to go ahead. Just where do we want to go? As I see it, we want to get greater security in living, greater education, greater social and political justice, greater moral fiber—*for everybody who will work, and for nobody else.*"

In Hoover's humanitarianism there is little room for psycho-analytical justifications of people who won't work or who insist upon living by crookedness. The idler and the criminal do not importantly come within his sympathetic activity. He had no boyhood experience of them.

His boyhood relatives and neighbors, while firmly believing that "the needs of the fatherless are to be supplied," were equally firm in the belief that if orphans would not work, "neither let them eat."

The nine-year-old orphan, Herbert Hoover, ate.

He accordingly worked at every sort of work of which a hearty boy with two hands and two feet would be capable, on a farm. I spare the reader the milking of the cows, the currying of the horses, the chopping of the fire-wood, the following of the mower, the fetching of jugs of water for hot hired men, the turning of the churn, the waking at dawn, the struggle between deathly sleepiness and a woman's voice uttering the mandate for one more—one more—chore at dusk. Having done it myself, I see nothing heroic about it, nothing distinctive. Millions upon millions upon millions of American boys have done it since Jamestown and Plymouth Rock. What is all this about "He was only a poor farm-boy"? What less artificially dulling education could there be? Or one that oftener spurs its recipients to gallop to a great distance away from poverty?

Andrew Hoover—six generations back—had been a farmer in Maryland and in North Carolina. His son John had been a farmer in North Carolina and in Ohio. John's son Jesse had been a farmer in Ohio. Jesse's son Eli had been a farmer in Ohio and in Iowa. Eli's son Jesse had wandered a bit into being a village blacksmith and a village purveyor of machines and tools. Jesse's son Herbert was now back at the ancestral habit of tilling the earth.

He labored at it under the kindly guidance of his uncle Allan Hoover, after whom—many years later—he was to name his own second

son. His transfer to his Uncle Allan's farm
meant a separation of only a few miles from his
birth-village of West Branch. It also meant,
however, a separation from his brother and
from his sister.

His brother was taken by another uncle. His
sister was taken by a grandparent. Herbert
Hoover's boyhood was to run the rest of its
course quite outside the comfortable confidence
that a boy normally derives from the mutually
protective household association of brother, sister, mother, father.

It is a tenable theory that this experience
either produced or accentuated one of the odd-
est paradoxes in his character. No man seeks
society more, and yet no man is more charged
with an essential unassuaged loneliness.

His business-offices ever since he left California on his recurrent trips to the Orient and
to Europe in 1897 have been thoroughfares to
the feet of men of all nations. His homes in
California, in London, in Washington, have
been alighting-spots for unceasing swarms of
friends—and strangers. He dines with people.
He lunches with people. He breakfasts with
people. I confidently believe that he has revolved among more people than any other man
alive. Yet in his continuous encirclement by
them he seems often almost at bay. He some-

times indeed looks at people as if he thought they might bite him. Or, like a cat in danger, he looks away from the danger as if to divert the enemy's gaze from himself to some neutral object. Hence his annoying habit—annoying to many visitors—of gazing not at them but at the floor or the molding.

Only among his most insistent familiars do the impeding leaves get all stripped off from this human psychological artichoke. Otherwise they all remain upon him, layer within layer within layer, unpeelable by others because unshedable by himself.

Widely thereupon the hasty and wholly erroneous conclusion is carried that Herbert Hoover "does not know people." The truth is that he knows people penetratingly and exhaustively well.

He has employed thousands of people for high and crucially important private and public efforts. Almost never has he picked a man who has failed in executive capacity. Almost never has he picked a man who has failed in personal loyalty. Hoover's subordinates almost invariably succeed. They almost invariably give him lifelong support in any design that he may then or thereafter embrace. The men who have been his aides in his multitudinous enterprises have not remained merely his "staff." They have

become—with far-reaching political consequences—his "gang." The adulation of some
of them for him is an incense so thick from the
thuribles which they swing before "The Chief"
that non-members of the cult are sometimes
borne out swooning.

It cannot possibly be said that a man with
such a genius for selecting successful executives
and with such a genius for selecting fanatically
faithful followers "does not know people." He
must—he does—know them through and
through.

In explanation then of his haltingness in manner toward most of them, one is driven—in part
—to the tentative theory that Hoover does not
yet wholly know himself. He may be hindered
in self-expression by a still imperfect self-
comprehension.

It is certain that, in so far as he has ever
found himself, he has found himself only gradually. There is no truth whatsoever in the bed-
time stories to the effect that when a baby he
crawled toward pebbles and rocks in pursuance
of an unconquerable determination to become a
great mining engineer. One of his most dis-
arming charms is his utter repudiation of all
romantic spurious tales about his legendary
young remarkableness. I have his own authority for stating that throughout his early

boyhood he gathered rocks with a completely thoughtless boyish irrelevancy and purposelessness.

He had no geological or engineering ambitions till they were suggested to him later—much later—by chance meetings with travelers and by groping readings of college catalogues. He had no intentions upon a career in Australia till a firm in London happened to send to an office in San Francisco—an office in which Hoover happened to be employed—a demand for an American mining expert. He had no effective stirrings within him toward public service till the accomplished accumulation of a private fortune had left him mentally bored and spiritually hungry. He is not an apparition. He is a growth. Nor has he yet to-day by any means ceased growing and changing.

Perhaps not until his growing pains are all over—perhaps not until he is wholly finished inside—will he ever be able to be wholly at ease with the world external.

It may—it may—be so. All that we can be truly sure of is that there does exist in him a most certain considerable personal inexpressiveness and that this trait was surely deepened by his early loss of the easy familiarities of home and his early subjection to the reticences and concealments inevitably induced by a life under alien roofs and in family circles related but strange.

Those circles followed fast one upon another. The orphan Herbert was soon snatched from his uncle Allan Hoover's farm in Iowa to his uncle John Minthorn's clearing in Oregon. Uncle John was a doctor and also a teacher, in addition to being a pioneer and a builder. At Newberg in Oregon there were trees to be chopped down, there was frontier house-keeping and yard-keeping to be done, there was the new Pacific Academy to be built, there were classes to go to, there were Uncle John's horses to prepare for their journeys to the houses of patients.

Here was continued work for Herbert Hoover, along with newer and wider opportunities for schooling. Here, in that latter respect, was growth—growth toward a more copious knowledge of the world of books. Much, perhaps, in Herbert Hoover's career, must be attributed to the luck which gave him, in his uncle John Minthorn, not only a protector but a professional educator.

The Quaker passion for education began now to twine itself in Hoover with the Quaker passion for work and for solvency.

Upon the point of solvency I was remarking once that Dr. Charles Frederick Holder in his history of "The Quakers in Great Britain and America" says:

"Among the Quakers a pauper would have been an impossibility."

Hoover, with his perfectly Quaker willingness to bring all things down from romance to reality, remarked in return:

"It's not surprising. If any man by his vices was on the way to pauperism, he stopped being a Quaker."

The Quakers lived under any economic system that happened to be prevalent in their neighborhood and nation. That system might plunge other whole communities into destitution and squalor. The Quakers emerged with treasure in heaven but with a margin still at their bankers' on earth. Rule Two of that wonderfully matter-of-fact code of spiritual living devised by the Quaker elders at Balby in England in 1656 was:

"Persons who walk disorderly are to be spoken to in private; then before two or three witnesses; then, if necessary, the matter is to be reported to the Church."

Rule Fifteen was:

"Debts to be punctually paid, that nothing may the Children of Light owe to any man but love to one another."

The little boy Herbert Hoover had an account book in which he entered all items of income and of outgo arising from his share of the estate of approximately fifteen hundred dollars left to him and to his brother and sister out of the prematurely shortened lives of their parents. He was inducted early into the sanctity of savings. He was given a set toward labor. He was given a set toward capital. In the Pacific Academy he was given a set toward what the Quakers always pile on top of earning: learning.

I apologize not at all for saying so much at this point about Quakerism. Quakerism was the prime mold of Hoover's character—and it remains so.

Hoover may still be seen sitting in the silence in a Quaker meeting-house in Washington. He likes the silence. His wife—not Quaker by origin—has come to like it equally. The Hoovers are Quakers by practice—and by ensuing abiding temper.

They begin all their thinking with the thought of "The Inner Light." That is, they start with the idea not of any external human authority but with the idea of some internal human—and yet supposedly divine and sacred—command.

It is immediately theoretically obvious—and

also in practice socially and historically true—
that such people will not, and do not, look first
to any collective or governmental precepts.
They take those precepts into realistic account,
but they necessarily look first to the promptings,
the discernments, the divinations, of the individual man and individual woman.

It will be forever vain for certain of our
"advanced progressives" to expect Hoover to
strive to erect among us any consolidated governmental mechanism which will transcend and
overwhelm the incalculable creative play of individual faith and fancy and adventure. It was
the Quaker in Hoover, far back of the business
man in Hoover, that led him to write a book not
on "American Social Progress" but on "American Individualism."

On this point Hoover's duties as Food Administrator in the United States during the
Great War have produced in some quarters a
certain deep misapprehension of his views. He
seemed then to stand forth primarily as a man
of regulations and restrictions. His own constant assertion was—to the contrary—that
those regulations and restrictions were purely
temporary expedients for the meeting of a situation fleeting and abnormal. His abiding policy
was stated on the very day after the proclama-
tion of the Armistice in 1918, when in words

well worth exact recollection now he said:
"Our work under the Food Control Act has
revolved largely around the curtailment of
speculation and profiteering. This Act will ex-
pire at the signing of the peace with Germany.
It represents a type of legislation justified only
under war conditions. It is my belief that the
tendency of all such legislation, except in war,
is in an over-degree to strike at the roots of
individual initiative. We have secured its execution during the war with the willing coöperation of ninety-five per cent. of the traders
of the country; but under peace conditions it
would degenerate into a harassing blue law."

"Blue law!" It is only in the course of a
choice between evils that Hoover accepts governmental coercion of people's purses or persons. He would prefer to feed the torch of
collective Liberty from the individual "Inner
Light." Individualism with him is not a mere
political theory. It is with him a religious
truth.

Contrariwise — or correspondingly — it is
wholly in vain for certain of our solid (or
stolid) "conservatives" to expect him to be
willing to surrender society at discretion to impersonal non-moral business forces. Economic
relations in Christian historic thought—and
very pointedly and poignantly in Christian

Quaker thought—are ethical relations. In the code of Balby it was even laid down, by a most extreme stretch of the principle of ethical fellowship, that no master among "the Children of Light" might put away his servant "but by the like consent of the servant." The Quaker urge is to fill all life, including political and economic life, with a broadening discovery of ethical obligations and requirements.

This sort of "progressiveness" is of the very essence of the Quaker nature. I once, with ears attuned to a quite different theological philosophy, heard Hoover comment upon his own as follows:

"If you live by an external precept, your temptation always is by your own thought to try to narrow it. If you live by a supposed inner light, your temptation is perhaps equal. It is to try—perhaps unduly—to spread it to cover more ground as your own thought covers more ground."

Hoover is in politics and economics an individualist, but an individualist forever putting upon individualism a heavier and heavier harness of ethics; and he can no more change this direction and tendency of his than he can change his memories of his long boyhood hours —then seemingly interminably long—in Quaker meeting-houses.

Nor, again, and in connection with that individualism, can he ever change his equalitarianism. In the Quaker meeting-house of his first recollection there was no clergy. There were no special "ministers." There was not even that concession to any outward conceivable inequality among men before God.

It followed from this theological equalitarianism that if negroes could be supposed to have souls, then negro slavery before God must be wrong. Hence the impermanency of the residence of Hoover's ancestors in North Carolina. They were moved to bear witness against slavery. Their witnessing against it having been disregarded and even scorned, they were moved to depart from that Egypt into a freer desert. They were moved also to make their recoil from slavery the springboard of their later politics.

They welcomed and joined the Republican Party. In Hoover's Quaker Iowa village of birth and of earliest boyhood there was just one Democrat. Everybody else was a Republican in direct consequence of the issue of slavery versus Quakerism.

Nor do the after-effects of Hoover's early religious experiences stop by any means at the line thus marked.

Born and bred an individualist, born and bred

a Republican, Hoover was born and bred also to be wholly blind to any alleged value in any artificial social discriminations between men and women.

It is true that up and down the middle of the Quaker meeting-house at West Branch, Iowa, there was a partition which separated the male from the female worshipers. It was perhaps a foot and a half or two feet high. It was quite inadequate as a destroyer of the visibility of Quaker damsels to the eyes of their suitors. It evidenced nevertheless a certain separation from the supreme earthly force in favor of concentration upon forces and powers above. It was in no aspect a discrimination against the female element in the congregation. For observe!

The partition proceeded from the rear to the front of the church and then ascended the rostrum, producing an area for women in the leadership of the congregation's affairs as well as an area for men. In the men's area there sat "elders." In the women's area there also sat "elders."

Hoover's great-grandmother, Rebecca, in whose presence he felt the awesome power of extreme but vigorous and commanding age, was an "elder." His mother, Huldah, was not only an "elder" but a most special and accepted

vehicle of exhortations to the faithful—and to
the faltering.

She was a woman of a gentle and serene
piety, much given to prayer, and deriving from
prayer many messages which she preached to
those about her. Since she was "moved by the
spirit," these messages of hers were thought
just as valid as if they had been communicated
to her husband or to any other male. Her sex
was not in question. There was no thought in
that community of what Thorstein Veblen has
so delightfully satirically called "the Levitical
inadequacy of women." There was no thought
of their ineligibility to the priesthood. If God
called them to be "priests," they were
"priests"; and the congregation listened to
them with sexless respect and acceptance.

Hoover's mother preached not only in the
meeting-house at West Branch but also—for
her widely reported power of transmission of
spiritual instruction—in many other meeting-
houses elsewhere. In her widowhood she thus
traveled much. She almost, as it were, had a
roving "charge," like a Methodist "circuit-
rider." She was, in truth and in actual effect, a
"minister"—a "minister" not indeed by ordination but fully by the ancient Quaker equivalent of ordination: common consent.

Naturally she was venerated in her husband's

house as well as in the meeting-houses of her
sect. It was a veneration accompanied, indeed,
by the Quaker doubleness of grip which never
loses this world in aspiring to the other. Her
husband, Jesse, who had a talent for humor,
was delighted to plague her with whimsicalities
which her serious mentality could not quite
catch. He could tease a prophet of God, and
did. Yet a prophet she was, and so recognized,
and so, therefore, in a sense, "set apart" as a
special "vessel of grace," with authority to
teach "The Word," as fully as if she had been
a man.

The political consequences of such an environment were clear and were irresistible. If the
Quaker faith demanded freedom for negroes, it
equally demanded suffrage for women. If
equality dwelt in the tabernacle of God, there
was certainly no reason why it should not dwell
also in the polling-booth. Hoover, I should say,
deserves scant applause—or scant censure—for
his automatic acceptance of the presence, and
of the potential power, of women in our public
life. Not through the whole of his earliest and
most formative years did he ever see any negation of that presence or any negation of that
potential power in either of the two dominant
phases of his young life: home and church.

Individualism, Republicanism, suffragism:

those three things are politically in Hoover as much by blood as by brain. To them must be added a fourth: a leaning—sometimes politically a quite damaging leaning—toward peace.

Quakers are known to the world principally through their peacefulness. To most non-Quakers the Quaker religion seems to be pivoted on peace. That is a misconstruction of it. The primitive pivot of the Quaker religion is the literal whole of The Gospels. Peacefulness is but a portion of that whole. It nevertheless is indeed a portion and it was diligently pursued in West Branch and in all of Springdale Township, within which West Branch is situated.

Springdale Township was a Quaker township; and Mr. Cyrenus Cole, Member of Congress from the Iowa Fifth District and authoritative author of "A History of the People of Iowa," tells me out of his antiquarian researches that "for thirty years no one in Springdale Township was arrested; for no one there violated the laws of either God or man."

This peacefulness and lawfulness affected even "the younger generation" in West Branch. It affected even boys in short pants. They played much but they fought little.

There was no dearth in their lives of unbloody amusement and merriment; for they were not instructed to live sourly; and they could skate and bat balls and race their sleds without reproof and indeed with applause; but physical belligerent encounters among them were rare.

To strike a playmate was flatly—and without much hope of extenuation—a sin.

It is possible to trace to this early training a certain great political fault, or misfortune, in Hoover's adult temperament. Hoover is distressed by the personal attacks with which politics is always—and inevitably—accompanied.

He never personally attacks others. He is amazed, outraged, upset, when they attack him.

To indurated Washingtonians, who can without a quiver hear one another accused of everything from cheating one's baby brother out of his inheritance to stealing old mantel-pieces out of the basement of the Capitol, Hoover's behavior when he is under the tiniest drum-fire of personal charges seems ignominious and ridiculous.

He actually minds those charges. He collects the clippings containing them. He broods over them. He sends emissaries to his attackers to explain the righteousness of the events which they have misinterpreted. He does everything except the one thing that Washington could understand. He does everything except attack

his attackers and charge them with something
worse than the things with which they have
charged him.

"Counter-attack or else ignore." That is the
Washingtonian professional rule. Once Mr.
Hoover's peculiar sort of unavenging restive-
ness under attacks was brought to Mr. Coolidge's attention. He perused some of the
attacks and then remarked to a friend:

"Can it be that Mr. Hoover is disturbed by
these?"

"Weren't you disturbed," inquired the friend
rather indignantly, "by that magazine attack
on you which the Democrats reprinted in the
last campaign?"

"What attack?" asked Mr. Coolidge.

It was specified.

"Oh," said Mr. Coolidge, "I remember. The
magazine had a green cover. I started reading
the article, but it was against me; so I quit."

That cold indifference, rising to its sublimest
known recorded altitude in Mr. Coolidge, can
freeze an attacker. A sudden right to the jaw
can paralyze him. Hoover pursues neither
course. Unable to adopt recrimination, he is
equally unable to escape feeling astonishment
and resentment.

He simply was never habituated in boyhood
to combative roughness. The pain he did not

suffer then he accumulates—for compensation —now. When hit, he can neither genuinely laugh nor genuinely retaliate. He simply genuinely suffers, and then simply, peacefully and scientifically labors to establish his innocence.

An advantage for him may some day, it is true, emerge from the fact that nobody ever will be able to remember any personal outrage committed by Hoover upon friend or upon enemy. Hoover has blackened nobody's reputation, assassinated nobody's character, nobody's at all. His political inoffensiveness may some day more than counter-balance his lack of skill in political self-defense.

Meanwhile, however, his distress and dismay before ordinary normal political libel and slander is surely to be regarded as a political disadvantage of considerable bulk and burden.

It must not be thought, nevertheless, that it is always possible to bait a Quaker with complete continued impunity. The teachings of the Quakers regarding combat seem to have some sort of occasional elasticity. Hoover's father was too young for the Civil War, but there were uncles of Hoover's who fought all the way through it. Also, from out of the Quaker community of Springdale Township, there came recruits to the Lilliputian extravaganza "army" which John Brown in 1859 led to Harper's

Ferry to assault the battlements of "The Slave Power."

Brown, passing and re-passing through Iowa on his way between Kansas and the East, drilled his men for a time on a Springdale Township farm. There he was joined by Edwin and Barclay Coppoc, Quaker sons of a Quaker widow. They advanced to being in the forefront of his little handful of final combatants. Barclay escaped back from Harper's Ferry to Iowa, a fugitive from the lower, if not from the higher, law. Edwin ascended the gallows and was dropped to infamy and to the coming marching songs of the soldiers of the Union.

Non-resistance is certainly not always unanimous among Quakers. Services of mercy in the midst of battle are customary commonplaces among them. They are not accused of cowardice. They nevertheless not only prefer peace but are ready and impetuous converts to plans for the organized international perpetuation of peace. In a subsequent chapter I shall mark what befell the hero of this narrative in the matter of the League of Nations. It betrayed him into a gross aberration from the true political tenor of his career. I here observe only that the twig which grew up to be the tree of that aberration at Paris and at Washington was bent in the unoffending and unarrested

Quaker peacefulness of West Branch, Iowa.

These political considerations, on the point of individualism, on the point of Republicanism, on the point of suffragism, on the point of peacefulness, were naturally in Hoover's boyhood quite unapprehended by him in comparison with the two immediate Quaker duties which I have already mentioned: the duty to labor and the duty to get educated.

The Quakers, though a tiny folk numerically, had produced Haverford College in Pennsylvania in 1830, Earlham College in Indiana in 1847, Swarthmore College in Pennsylvania in 1864, Penn College in Iowa in 1873. Hoover's elder brother Theodore went to Penn.

There was a tradition in West Branch of a Quaker woman who, upon being left a widow with seven young children, a team of horses, and one hundred and sixty acres of utterly unbroken prairie, and with nothing else, stood beside her husband's grave and said:

"Each one of the children shall have a university education."

Hoover's mother took in sewing in her widowhood to keep her thin purse meagerly replenished; but it would seem that the idea of a steadily ascending education for the children was with her and with them a sort of automatic accepted prospect which no paucity of financial resources could extinguish or really even dim.

Education was in the air of the community and in the temper of the family. Hoover's Uncle Laban was concerned with the education of Indians in what was then the Indian Territory. Hoover's Uncle John, who received him at Newberg, Oregon, in his twelfth year, in 1886, was diligently laboring at the scholastic foundations of the "academy" which was to become Pacific College in 1891.

In that "academy" Hoover, in his fourteenth or fifteenth year, was inducted into his "secondary" or "high school" education. Yet almost immediately his educational development was again interrupted by work.

His Uncle John moved from Newberg to the neighboring town of Salem in order to enter the business of the Oregon Land Company. He took Hoover with him, naturally; and Hoover proceeded to do chores in and about the real-estate office in Salem, just as he had done chores in and about the "academy" in Newberg.

He seems not to have been sorry to make the shift. With all of his passion for the ladder of education toward broader and better opportunities, he seems to have exhibited thoroughly an ordinary boy's attitude toward immediate "lessons." Asked once which one of his studies interested him most in his boyhood, he answered curtly and unflinchingly:

"None."

Deep designs were not in him at that time. It is to be gathered that his only really decisive and purposive notion then was that somewhere and somehow there was a way up, and that he would take it.

The office-boy job at Salem was Hoover's first touch with business. A tale of that time—perhaps true—perhaps not—is soundly based on one of Hoover's earliest and most enduring characteristics. One night, it is said, a group of his uncle's customers sat in his uncle's office and conversed at cross-purposes and with a complete lack of results hour after hour. Hoover terminated the proceedings by creeping unobserved into a dark corner and turning off the whole supply of gas-light. Darkness brought silence—and dispersal to bed.

If Hoover did not do this, he should have done it, and he might have. No measures are with him too extreme for the curtailing of undue talk. Conferences which contain aimless and irrelevant remarks, and which protract themselves beyond the reaching of decisions, are to him a horror. Since, however, he holds

conferences every day, and since virtually all
conferences contain aimless and irrelevant remarks and protract themselves beyond the
reaching of decisions, it is manifest that he has
to be horrified and excruciated a large part of
the time. He would undoubtedly be happier if
he had a little more tolerance of cross-country
off-track human loquacity.

It has to be said, however, that the curtailment of speech which he would wish to impose
upon others he imposes perfectly impartially
upon himself. Victor Lawson, publisher of the
Chicago *Daily News,* once wired his Washington correspondent to say: "If there is no news,
cut it short." If Hoover has nothing to say, he
cuts it so short that there is nothing of it at all.

He can come home and sit at his table among
visitors and tell tales the whole evening long.
He can at other times come home and sit at his
table among visitors and say virtually nothing
at all throughout dinner except polite variants
upon "yes" and "no." He is—in a way—a
Quaker meeting enlarged to all of the days of
the week. If the spirit moves him, he speaks.
If not, principally not. It would be no great
deprivation to him if he were condemned to a
literal observance of that rocky and thorny text
which accompanies the beatitudes of the Ser-
mon on the Mount:

"Let your communication be, Yea, Yea; Nay, Nay; for whatsoever is more than these cometh from evil."

That text was much hurled about among Hoover's ancestors. It quite occasionally to-day rebounds upon his friends.

We so far have been considering Hoover principally as the offspring of a certain stock, the nursling of a certain group, the resultant of a certain inherited and inescapable parallelogram of forces. We now come to certain accidents— and thereupon simultaneously to certain youthful buddings of his own proper distinctive energies and ambitions.

One day, at Newberg, or at Salem, there arrived a stranger—unseen previously by Hoover, unseen by him afterwards, unknown to him now. This stranger discoursed upon the difference between, on the one hand, merely working and, on the other hand, having a profession. He discoursed in particular upon the glamors and emoluments of the profession of mining. He discoursed, and passed on. He came out of the dark and went into the dark but left behind him in a boy's mind a light that was to glow in many countries.

This new light began to warm into a purpose. The boy began presently to read the catalogues of universities in which scientific training could especially be secured.

He accordingly discarded from his calculations the otherwise compelling claims of the colleges of the Quakers. He wanted an institution of learning in which science would be more prominent. He decided that he had found it in an institution which was not yet opened but which was soon to give world-wide currency to the name of Leland Stanford.

He was beginning now to have his own ideas, to form his own intentions, to break away—a bit —a little bit—from his heritage.

He did it with a forthrightness and—in truth —a quiet but convinced "nerve" which were soon to display themselves as among the dominating springs of his success. He proceeded at Portland—to take the Leland Stanford entrance examinations.

He failed. He perfectly naturally and necessarily failed. It is sometimes said to be noteworthy that Hoover was able to enter Stanford at the age of seventeen. It is much more noteworthy that he was able to intrude himself into Stanford with a preparation as fragmentary and as inadequate as his most certainly was.

He had little Latin. He had no Greek. He had no modern language. He had some mathematics. He had some physiology, expanded on

Sunday afternoons by a contemplation of
charts of stomachs ruined by alcohol on exhibition at meetings of the Newberg Quaker Band
of Hope. He was thoroughly educated as to the
effects of alcohol. Otherwise, in the spring of
1891, at the age of sixteen, he was about as far
from being a scholastic prodigy as would have
been fitting in any intelligent boy brought up
with his rough-and-ready but wholly wholesome
and quite beckoning educational opportunities.

What saved him, at Portland, in the darken-
ing aftermath of his failure to pass the Stanford examinations, was the accident of the personality of the examiner.

The examiner was Professor Swain, head of
Stanford's prospective Department of Mathematics, head afterwards of Swarthmore College,
a noticing man, and a Quaker, and kindly. He
has since communicated to Dr. Vernon Kellogg,
of Stanford and of the National Academy of
Sciences, our first authentic report of Hoover
the youth as seen by an experienced and responsible observer. Professor Swain, in spite
of Hoover's bad showing in the examinations,
told him to come to Palo Alto and to plunge into
Stanford's first freshman class because:

"I observed that he put his teeth together
with great decision, and his whole face and
posture showed his determination to pass the

examinations at any cost. He evidently was summoning every pound of energy he possessed to answer correctly the questions before him. I was naturally interested in him. On inquiry I learned that he had studied only two books of Plane Geometry, and was trying to solve an original problem based on the fourth book. While he was unable to do this, he did much better; for the intelligence and superior will he revealed in the attempt convinced me that such a boy needed only to be given a chance. So although he could not pass all of the tests, I told him to come to my rooms at the hotel after the examinations, as I would like to talk with him. He came promptly at the appointed hour with a friend of his, the son of a banker in Salem, Oregon. The two boys invited me and Mrs. Swain to stop at Salem to visit them, which we did. I learned there that Herbert Hoover, for that was the boy's name, was an industrious, thoughtful, ambitious boy earning his own living while he studied.''

In this account of young Hoover by Professor Swain there is a conspicuous absence of all such words as ''clever'' and ''brilliant.'' The boy was ''industrious.'' He worked. He was ''thoughtful.'' He could concentrate. He was ''ambitious.'' He could leap at a hurdle without even any properly prepared ground for a take-off.

Palo Alto then in the summer of 1891 got a student studying very hard to get one more chance to enter Stanford with its first entrants.

Hoover's family, generation after generation, had sought new clearings. It was appropriate enough that he should go to a university where the workmen had not yet completed the buildings within which

"The fair sum of six thousand years'
Traditions of civility"

could be housed.

While the workmen worked, Hoover worked —particularly at mathematics, and even more particularly at English.

He then took the Stanford entrance examinations again. This time he passed, and was admitted. He carried with him, however, one extremely significant and characteristic partial failure. He entered Stanford "conditioned" in English. He had not been able to bring his mind to an academic mastering of words and of the forms and relations of words.

Deficient then in words as objects of study, deficient also in words as vehicles of self-expres-

sion, younger than almost any other freshman,
shyer than almost any other human being on the
whole campus, tall, lean, slightly stoopy, awk-
ward, hardened to work, hardened to poverty,
hardened to the exigent morals of the Quaker
sect, resistant internally to every new environment, determined and destined to seek new environments without pause, concealing beneath
a shrinking sensitiveness an almost overween-
ing confidence and courage, a puzzle perhaps
to himself, a blank certainly for many ensuing
months to others, Hoover in the fall of 1891
was by some luck and much nerve a "college
man."

At his entrance into Stanford there was capital in Hoover's pocket. It amounted to three
hundred dollars. He husbanded it. He took
immediate employment as a temporary clerk to
the University Registrar. He sought and found
other campus employments throughout all his
autumns and winters and springs at Palo Alto.
In his summers he worked in the wilds.

His first long vacation was bestowed upon the
Ozarks. His Stanford Professor of Geology—
Dr. Branner—was also the Arkansas State
Geologist. Through him Hoover was engaged
to carry a transit and to do other useful sub-

ordinate labor in connection with Ozark eleva-
tions and contours.

In succeeding long vacations he took to the
field in the service of the Geological Survey of
the Federal Government. He thus early combined scientific research with an enlightening
experience of governmental methods.

He learned, for instance, that all governmental property must be accounted for and that
the accounting must be in accordance with reason as understood at Washington. He learned
this most particularly in consequence of the
demise of a horse.

There was no doubt that the horse was dead.
He had been tethered for the night a short distance away from camp. In the morning Hoover
proceeded toward him to prepare him for the
day's march. The scene disclosed was sad and
was also highly provocative of conjecture. The
horse lay lifeless with his tethering rope twisted
around both his neck and the fetlock of his
right hind leg.

Hoover summoned a colleague. The two of
them observed, and reflected. They came to an
identical conclusion. This conclusion they put
into full legal form just as soon as their travels
could carry them to a village in which a notary
public was available. They put it into a solemn
and sworn affidavit addressed to the Geological

Survey in the District of Columbia. The horse had died of strangulation induced by an effort on his part to scratch his right ear with his right hind foot, in the course of which effort he had unwittingly and unwarily enveloped his neck in coils of his tethering rope and had thus by the said coils come to his end.

Hoover dispatched the affidavit to Washington and thought no more of the incident. His unconcern was dissipated when in due course he received from Washington an official communication informing him that the value of the horse was now a lien upon his salary. The Government would admit that possibly the horse was dead. It would most certainly not admit that the horse could have died in the manner reported. Experts had been consulted. Their reports were unanimous to the effect that horses do not scratch their right ears with their right hind feet. Therefore the claim for the loss of the horse would be disallowed, and the Government would expect to be reimbursed for that loss by the person finding and reporting it—namely, Mr. Hoover.

Vainly did Hoover and his immediate chief, Waldemar Lindgren, seek experts of their own —veteran veterinarians—who were ready to testify, and who did testify, that it was within

the nature of a horse to attempt to use his
right hind foot for the scratching of his right
ear. Governmentally it remained scientifically
established and held that no horse ever did do
it and that no horse ever would. For that accident to that horse therefore the Government
never would—and never did—pay. It successfully laid the cost upon the dead animal's
wholly guiltless guardians.

In the relations between government and citizen it is by no means always the citizen that
does the cheating. Hoover had early reason to
note that fact in the nature of governments—
all around the world.

The climax to Hoover's labors as a federal
geologist in college vacation-times arrived when
he assisted in a survey of the region lying near
Lake Tahoe upon the border between California
and Nevada. For mapping purposes the Federal Geological Survey divides the territory of
the United States into little areas called "quad-
rangles." One of these areas—near Lake Tahoe—is called "the Pyramid Peak Quadran-
gle." When the map of it was officially printed,
with all its wonderful lines (straight and wig-
gly) to express all its remarkable features, artificial and natural, Hoover saw with a first
bounding throb of professional creative joy that

his own name had been entered on the map margin to indicate his own personal part in the masterly performance.

It is not without meaning that Hoover's first contribution to the world's literature was not a poem. It was not an essay. It was a map.

In his classes on the campus Hoover made excellent progress in the studies leading toward more maps and toward more explorations of the earth. His idea of a "liberal education" in the first semester of his first year was that he should study—and he did study—advanced algebra, linear and free-hand drawing, and shopwork in mechanics. Above all, he pushed out —far out—into geology and its great historic and prehistoric lines and levels and layers under the guidance of Dr. Branner's knowledge and—what is more—Dr. Branner's wisdom.

Dr. Branner believed in science—pure science —as the start even toward practical action. He believed in thinking as a guide even toward doing. He thought that mine-bosses would presently teach young Hoover a thoroughly sufficient plenty about the manual operation of jacks and drills. As for himself, he grounded young Hoover not in the application of science but in science itself; for he knew full well that the opportunity for the application was stretching spaciously ahead.

To Dr. Branner, many years afterwards, out of a home-turning exile in England, Hoover dedicated the English translation which he and Mrs. Hoover had made of the immense sixteenth-century Latin work of Georgius Agricola on the digging and smelting of metals.

The full truth is that Dr. Branner took a boy who might possibly have been only a mining engineer and made him also—and first—a scholar. By scholarship in science he turned him ultimately even toward a scholarly assault upon old verbal strata in the history of mining.

Was much of the mining lore of the Middle Ages buried in the strangely invented Latin words of Georgius Agricola? Hoover—with Mrs. Hoover—dug down into those words with philology called now to the aid of metallurgy. That English translation of Agricola's "De Re Metallica" is a labor of infinitely toilsome linguistic learning. To mention a gross detail, the book which contains it weighs six and a half pounds. It was done to amuse what Mr. and Mrs. Hoover with unconscious levity call their "leisure hours." It was done while Hoover was director of mining operations involving hundreds of thousands of men on four continents. It was a mark—accompanying many other marks yet to be recorded—of the fact that back of the practical in Hoover there has always been, ever since he knew Branner, a strong streak of the academic and an abiding faith in the science that seems to have no purpose but curiosity, comprehension, culture.

In Stanford, however, almost to the very end of his undergraduate days, he suffered greatly —and unavailingly and defeatedly—from the crotchety requirements of the rules of college English composition. He never could quite see why an ability to spell and to parse and to punctuate "correctly" should be piled on top of an ability to transmit one's ideas intelligibly. It was the ideas that interested him. He could not yet focus himself upon what he regarded as the mere clothing and tailoring of the ideas.

Even to-day it cannot be said that English style is his forte. Style is an art. Hoover's mind is not—in the ordinary sense of the word —an "artistic" mind. It is indeed a civilized mind. It is indeed a highly cultivated mind. It perceives—that is—the speculations of life as well as its activities, its calls to understanding as well as its calls to action. Few men have a greater refinement of mind than Hoover. His route to it, however, is not through the arts. It is through the sciences. It is on avenues along which words are laggards.

I confidently believe that he is among those few persons—few in civilization—who can think

really without the aid of words. Thought comes
to him, and even action often comes to him, before the words can mentally form themselves.
Most people, telephoning, will write words on
handy pieces of paper, if they write at all.
Hoover, telephoning, or talking, does not write
words. He writes lines, straight lines, curved
lines, lines in progressions and patterns.

These patterns are sometimes genuinely beautiful. There is "artistic" design in them.
They indicate a mind which, in its medium, has
a sense of abstract creative construction. The
method remains that of mere lines—exploring,
engineering, lines. The result will lie on a piece
of paper before him without a word that explains, or that could explain. He has not been
thinking verbally. He has been thinking
linearly.

He accordingly was far from distinguishing
himself at Stanford in language. Having been
"conditioned" in English upon entrance, he
took English in his freshman year and failed to
pass it. He took it again in his sophomore and
junior and senior years and again in each of
those successive years failed to pass it. He at
last wrote a supreme essay in paleontology.
The professor of paleontology—J. P. Smith—
was greatly struck by it. He was so much
struck by it that he inserted into it all the punc-

tuation and grammar that Hoover had left out. He then took it to the professor of English. The professor of English was vastly pleased with the mentality disclosed in the essay; and Hoover was held to have met the requirements for graduation in paleontology and English together.

Hoover, it will be seen, was decidedly not what is called an "all-around student." In fact, Dr. Vernon Kellogg relates that Hoover, as a student, had a certain "disconcerting habit." "He would start in on a course and then, if he found it unpromising as a contribution to the special education in which he was interested, he would simply drop out of the class without consultation or permission."

He acquired in college, in the end, just two eminences. He shone at paleontology, at geology, at the studies leading directly toward his profession. He acquired eminence on the path toward science. He also—and really much more importantly for his coming career—acquired an altitudinous eminence on the path toward personal leadership.

But that second path—in essence—was politics. How could a lad so diffident, so poor in the outward sparkle of personality, arrive at any success in the most brutally personal of all politics: the politics of an undergraduate body?

John Adams remarks somewhere in his writings that even in his callowest youth he had gained a firm grip on the proposition that personal popularity is not essential to political preferment. He fought with pretty nearly everybody he ever met, and became President.

Hoover was not personally unpopular, however, with his fellow-students. His difficulty lay deeper. He seemed—at the start—colorless. He was handicapped by the most genuinely fatal of all political impediments: inconspicuousness.

It took him a long time to survive it. He indeed never survived it much in the matter of recognition by clapping hand or yelling throat on the campus scene. Mr. Will Irwin, who entered Stanford while Hoover was still in it, records the relative silence that greeted Hoover's public appearances while other Senior-class heroes were getting cheered and chaffed by the tumultuous bleachers. Yet Hoover, at that very moment, was the elected—and also the obeyed—despot of the whole business management of all student-body activities.

He had entered into the politics of the matter, in the spring of his sophomore year, by being, as we have seen, a sort of precinct-worker for that young Progressive "Sosh" in the course of "Sosh's" proletarian ambitions to become

student-body President. It was Hoover's as-
signed duty, as has been pointed out, to arouse
the very dregs of the ''populace'' and the very
rinsings of the ''rabble''—those who lived in
''The Camp'' and who cooked their own meals
and who were destined probably to be high
executives later on for high-hand railroads and
for high-hat trusts—and to hurl them against
the pretensions and oppressions of the college's
Greek-letter aristocrats.

Hoover could speak well on that theme. His
Quaker individualism predisposed him, as it
still predisposes him, against cliques, combinations, monopolies. His Quaker equalitarianism
made him laugh then, as he laughs still, at social assumptions. He was a non-Greek-letter
man and a ''barb'' not only by fact but by farthest fancy and by conviction.

''Sosh,'' as it happened, was elected. The
Presidency of the student-body passed to the
plebs. Yet the victory was not properly complete. The patricians still held the minor offices.
The social revolution was yet to be perfected.

In the succeeding year—Hoover's junior year
—the mighty plans for the perfecting of it were
undertaken. There developed, naturally, the
need for a ''platform.'' It seemed that it was
not quite enough to promise the overthrow of
the lofty. What would the lowly do—what

would they actually practically do—when they had been elevated to the holding of all of the offices and of all power and authority?

It is a matter of indubitable college tradition that at this critical juncture Hoover put forth the first flowers of his enormous subsequent crop of reports, analyses, statistics, revelations of waste and plans for scientific orderliness.

His "platform" was economic, an appeal to the purse, a call to sobriety and solvency. It charged the patricians—truly enough—with laxity in financial administration, and it promised to supplant their casual and jovial supervision of student activities with a system of precise responsibilities, scrutinies, expense-accounts, ledgers, bank-books, and audits. At the center of that new horrific web there would sit a Treasurer (bonded, of course) who would absorb every nickel that was garnered up from the public by any student-activity—even of guitars and of mandolins—and who would thereupon never disburse a cent of it except upon a voucher, signed and verified.

Hoover had already gained a wide quiet reputation for solid sense. He was now hailed—or denounced—as a young man of lofty constructive imagination. Moreover, as was perfectly natural, Hoover's "barb" colleagues at once said to him:

"Since you were the only man who was capable of giving birth to this idea, you are the only man who shall bear the burden of nursing it. You are our candidate for Treasurer."

Thence came Stanford's most historic political ticket—most historic not only for recollection in fact but for embroidery by legend. It was the Three-H Ticket: Hinsdale for President, Hoover for Treasurer, Hicks for Manager of the Football Team.

No other equal political struggle is supposed ever to have happened on the Stanford campus. There was electioneering, they say, in those days, in Palo Alto. Every voter was located, solicited, impelled to the polls. The outcome was a memorable triumph for democracy and accounting. The Three H's won. The Greek alphabet was trailed in the dust along with the Roman Senate, Charles the First, and other enemies of "the people."

Throughout the whole of Hoover's last year in Stanford, therefore, the undergraduate student-body had a wholly "people's" government. Like almost every other "people's" government in history, it missed its major revolutionary purpose and accomplished, instead, a confirming and a strengthening of the business structure of society.

Fraternities continued. Social distinctions remained. "Queeners" still flaunted themselves. Boys with poor clothes still felt themselves abashed by girls in finery. Likes still flocked to likes. Unlikes still recoiled from one another. The democracy of a community all Quaker-gray, like West Branch, did not get adopted by a multicolored worldly world, like Stanford.

It was true that the "people's champions," raised to office, became famous. They governed. They were now among "the great ones of the earth." Yet, somehow, their elevation did not level the fate of all beneath them. Society still contained "society"; and the virtues of the "barbs" still confronted the fripperies of the "frats."

It was as large a lesson as could have been learned from an election as broad as the whole country or the whole globe. So was the additional lesson that accompanied it.

The "people's" government of the boys and girls of Stanford in 1894-5 installed a system of business administration of student activities that has lasted, in essence, to this day. What started (and failed) as "revolution" ended (and succeeded) as "reform."

The central reformer, naturally, was Hoover,

as Treasurer. His exigence in the discharge of
his duties became a fountain of college yarns—
for awe, for laughter.

He was already by way of being a veteran at
the keeping of accounts. He had kept accounts
of his own tiny patrimony. He had kept accounts of the numerous little businesses in
which he had engaged for self-support during
his freshman and sophomore and junior years.
He had kept accounts for various groups of college friends who could not straighten out the
finances of their common enterprises for themselves. Headed toward being an engineer, he
was then, as afterwards, throughout his whole
long series of contacts with great engineering
enterprises, really dominantly a business man.

He brought it about that the business basis of
all of the student activities of Stanford became
a collegiate playground for training in social
financial honesty and accuracy. No money
taken in by any roving band of college players,
trading upon the name of Stanford, could
escape his outstretched fingers. No statement
of expenses incurred could relax those fingers,
unless backed by justice—and sometimes, it
must be recorded, not even then!

What the Federal Government had done to
Hoover in the matter of that strangled horse,
Hoover—I am sad to say—seems now to have

visited in whimsical kind upon his suffering undergraduate fellow-citizens.

I summon, as a witness against him, Lester Hinsdale, then President of the student-body, now a Hoover Republican National Convention delegate from California. Hinsdale spent $8.50 going from Palo Alto to San Francisco to greet, officially, the University of Chicago visiting football team. Hoover disallowed the bill. He contended that Hinsdale should have been pleased, should have been proud, to represent Stanford upon that gigantic occasion with his own private resources. After an altercation of months he reduced Hinsdale to a tame accept-ance of $4.25.

He treated Will Irwin even more shamefully. Irwin has never printed it, but I have it from him.

Irwin came to college with a pair of football shoes which he had inherited at prep school from a friend. Hoover made him play in them, through the simple device of refusing to issue him any others. Then Irwin was injured and could play no longer. Hoover, however, found him wearing the shoes and demanded them. Irrelevantly, as Hoover looked at it, Irwin main-tained and proved that the shoes were his own private property. That contention Hoover, as Treasurer, could not hear. The shoes had been

used on the Stanford gridiron. He had seen
them there. They were therefore not private
but public property. He argued them off
Irwin's feet and added them to the college common store.

By such tyrannies, imposed and accepted
amid laughter, as well as by straightaway
honest system, Hoover developed the business
management of the student activities of Stanford from chaos and discontent into solvency
and social satisfaction. He was graduated a
great college "leader," memorable to the point
of myth in Stanford circles.

With all his want of preparation he had conquered the plaudits of his scientific teachers.
With all his want of outward expressiveness
he had conquered the suffrages of his undergraduate fellows. He had come a fleck of dull
dust. He was graduated a star.

A few months later—not because he "wanted
to get the experience"—not because he
"wanted to learn the business from the bottom up"—but precisely and only because he
could get no better job—he was pushing a
hand-car as a day-laborer in the dark and wet
drifts of a mine in the Sierras.

CHAPTER TWO

WORLD BUSINESS MAN

NINETEEN years later—in August of 1914—
there were more than one hundred thousand
Americans who were trying to flee homeward
out of Continental and British ports from before the terror of the onrush of the Great War.

Mr. Hoover, in that month of that year, was
living in London. He was living in the rented
habitation customarily his during his tarryings
in London—the quite historic house called "The
Red House," on Hornton Street. He had an
office in London on the street called Englishly
London Wall.

He had an office also in New York. He had
one also in San Francisco.

His business had required offices for him
also in Melbourne and in Sydney, Australia;
in Shanghai and in Tientsin, China; in Auck-
land, New Zealand; in Singapore, Malay Penin-
sula; in Rangoon and in Mandalay, Burma; in
Petrograd, Russia.

He was a responsible director in more than a
score of mining companies engaged in the operating of properties in Australia, Asia, Africa,

Europe and the Americas. He was the managing director—the immediate chief executive—of half a dozen of these companies. He was a constant consultant in the reviving and stabilizing of numerous other companies devoted to the extraction of metals and minerals from the earth.

He was rich. It was his second time at being rich. His first fortune had in some considerable part been taken away from him by the behavior of a partner whose personal deviations from financial rectitude became for Hoover personal financial liabilities for himself. That incident was wholly now in the past. Hoover was in the full flight now of his second fortune and in the full development of his own unimpeded business.

The Americans fleeing homeward, through London, attracted his gaze. They attracted from him something else, too.

How often had he himself hastened across the Atlantic, or across the Pacific, to seek, along with a tour of duty in his San Francisco office, a few days or a few months in a California home!

In 1902, when zinc and lead had taken him to Australia and gold and copper had taken him to New Zealand, he had found time nevertheless to build for Mrs. Hoover, at Monterey, California, a cottage which Mrs. Hoover could perhaps occupy when she was not—as usually—accompanying him on his errands abroad.

How extensive—and how protracted—those errands had been!

They had taken him first—in the third year after his graduation from Stanford—in 1897—when he was but twenty-three—to Australia, to its western region, to the gold deposits clustered about Coolgardie and Kalgoorlie.

In 1899 they had added China to his field of exploration and of management.

In 1901 he had followed the call of the drift and the pick into Japan.

In 1902 he first saw the underground resources of New Zealand.

In 1903, while retaining his connections and interests in the countries in which he had already labored and directed, he first saw the old metalliferous workings of India.

In 1904 he continued westward and arrived as organizer and re-organizer in Rhodesia and the Transvaal in Southern Africa.

In 1905 he established contacts and possessions in Egypt.

In 1907 he piled on top of these demands a fresh duty toward new developments which he planted and guided in Burma, in the Malay States, in Ceylon.

In 1908 he for the first time added the European Continent to Australia and Asia and Africa in the circling whirl of his professional travels. In that year he engineered and managed in Italy.

In 1909 he penetrated Russia to the Urals at Kyshtym, to the south of Ekaterinburg; and on a private estate half as big as Maryland, belonging to a branch of the Romanoff family and containing 75,000 tenants and workmen, he established new plants for iron, steel, coal, coke, lumber, sulphuric acid, copper—with railroads and with ships to serve them.

In the same year he did his first searching for gold in Korea.

In the same year he did his first metallurgical work in Germany.

In the subsequent year he did his first metallurgical work in France.

In 1911 he went beyond the Urals into Russian Siberia, to the south of Omsk, on the edge of the Baraba Steppe, hard by the beginnings of Tartary and Mongolia, and began the constructing of some fifteen or twenty river-steamers and the building of some two hundred miles of railroad to carry American mining machinery in, and to fetch Siberian natural resources out.

For five years his central physical task was a virtually annual circumnavigation of the globe. He had his office then principally on ships. He started eastward, or westward, and worked at his reports and his calculations on shipboard till he arrived at the first country of his quest. There he examined the properties for which he was responsible and then took ship again and worked again in his cabin-office, ever moving, eastward or westward, round and round, across all the seas, with "homeward bound" hauled down only to give place at once—once more—to "outward bound."

With what results externally? A fortune. With what results inwardly? They show in a letter he wrote at about that time to a friend.

The friend had consulted him about the ambitions of a young American who wished to go abroad. The friend had given to those ambitions some discouragement. Hoover wrote to him to say:

"DEAR BANCROFT:

"I was very glad to get your note. I have often thought you were right, though for other reasons than you mention.

"The American is always an alien abroad. He can never assimilate. Nor do other peoples ever accept him otherwise than as a foreigner.

"His heart is in his own country. Yet there is less and less of a niche for him when he returns.

"One feels that one should have built one's fortune in America. It might have been less imposing. Yet one would be among one's own people; and the esteem that one hopes to build among one's associates would not be wasted by leaving it and them behind, only to go home later and then try to build at it again."

With such feelings Hoover, in August of 1914, saw London crowded with unhappy Americans—unhappy because of the discomforts and losses of their flight from the war-scene—but homeward bound, happy.

Hoover was presently to take a hand in their affairs—at considerable ultimate cost to his own affairs.

But what had made his own affairs prosper so promptly?

One of the reasons was his own promptness— the same promptness that had led him to attempt the Stanford entrance examinations, in spite of imperfect schooling, just as soon as a determination to enter Stanford had come into his mind and will.

Leaving Stanford, he had pushed a hand-car at day wages in the Mayflower Mine at Grass

Valley in Northern California in 1895 till pushing it had inspired him.   The inspiration was a
characteristic one.   It was to seek the topmost
mining engineer within his reach.

That engineer was Louis Janin in San Francisco.   Hoover climbed out of his mine and went
to Janin's office.

Janin asked him for recommendations.   Hoover secured them readily.   He was always able
to rely upon the friendship of people who
closely and intimately had seen him actually at
work.   Among such people his special teacher
of geology at Stanford—Dr. Branner—was pre-
eminent both for his own character and for his
knowledge of Hoover's.

A recommendation which he once gave Hoover, while Hoover was yet an undergraduate,
says nothing about Hoover's mental ability but
says almost everything about what has made
that mental ability count.

"If," said Branner, "I told Hoover to start
to Kamchatka to-morrow morning to bring me
back a walrus tooth, I'd not hear of him or it
again till he came back with the tooth."

Branner recommended Hoover to Janin.
Janin offered to take him tentatively on.
Hoover gathered that his staying steadily on
might have something to do with typewriting.
He said he would be back Tuesday.   It was then

Friday. Emerging on to the street from Janin's office that Friday, says Dr. Vernon Kellogg, Hoover rented a typewriter. He reported for work at Janin's office on Tuesday an experienced typist.

He continued to have "luck." Janin happened to have a client whose interests were involved in a dispute which required a special knowledge of the geology of a certain part of the Sierras. Hoover happened, in the course of earning his living as an undergraduate and as a day-laborer, to have come into contact with that special knowledge. Janin was much pleased. He advanced Hoover from hanging about the office to inspecting and reporting in the field.

Hoover reported for Janin on mines in California, in Nevada, in New Mexico, in Arizona, in Colorado. Presumably he did it well; for Janin thereupon thrust him into an opening far beyond his years.

Here indeed was Hoover's supreme blow of "luck." There was in London a great international mining firm of the name of Bewick Moreing and Company. It had lately become interested in certain mines of gold in Western Australia. For the technical development of those mines it desired—wisely—an American engineer. Gold-mining in Australia had been stagnant. Gold-mining in America had been

active. It had also been progressive. Bewick
Moreing and Company wanted to introduce into
the Western Australian gold-fields the stimulating innovation of American machines and of
American methods. A letter from London
asked Janin to name the American engineer to
accomplish this large task.

Janin named Hoover. Hoover was then
twenty-three. It is alleged that Janin, in order
to make Hoover's candidacy more convincing,
told London that Hoover was thirty-five.

The job was one that might have daunted a
man of even that latter age. It might likewise
well have daunted anybody with Hoover's singular lack of joy in new scenes. Hoover is an
amazing mixture of a wanderer and a limpet.
In temper he loves to stick to a rock and be
washed only by familiar waves. In ambition he
turns sail-fish and forever swims into new seas
and into the company of new fishes, suffering
greatly while getting acquainted with them. He
grabbed the chance to go to Australia.

It was a decision of the most far-sighted—or
the "luckiest"—wisdom. The wisdom of it was
that of the old Scotchman who said to his son,
"There's lots of money to be made among the
English—by a Scotchman." In America Hoover would have been only one of many American
engineers. In Western Australia he was to be

one of few. In America he would have been only a small part of the knowledge of American mining technique. In Western Australia he was to be a dominating part of it. He went.

On his way, just as he had once improvised typewriting for Janin, he now started improvising age for Bewick Moreing and Company. He started growing a beard.

What he did in Australia, and what he learned, will be pertinent later. What is pertinent here is that he had not been in Australia much more than a year when Bewick Moreing and Company, like Janin, thrust him into an opportunity again far beyond his apparent growth.

In China there was a new régime within the Chinese Imperial Government. This régime was outwardly all bent toward modernity. It established, among other novelties, an Imperial Bureau of Mines. At the head of this Bureau it appointed an Imperial Director General of Mines. It now had a complete Mandarinic political machine for exploiting the supposedly limitless underground natural resources of China. All that it further needed was an engineer who would know just how to locate those resources and just how to bring them to the surface.

On this fairly vital last point it consulted

Bewick Moreing and Company. Bewick Moreing and Company could think of nobody better
qualified for pioneering in China than the
young American engineer who had made their
own pioneering pay—and pay profusely—in
Western Australia. The chore in Western Australia had been conquered. A friend in China
might be useful in the course of China's prospective colossal and giddy development. Bewick Moreing and Company recommended; and
Chang Yen Mao, Chinese Imperial Director
General of Mines, summoned; and Hoover went.

He was to save Chang Yen Mao's life for
him; and he was also to save for him his personal hold upon his private property; but there
was a little fleeting trip to California that had
to be made first.

Hoover got back to San Francisco in the
early days of February, 1899. He proceeded
to Monterey. Lou Henry lived there.

Miss Henry had been a freshman at Stanford
when Hoover was a senior. It might be an
exaggeration to say that she had been the object
of "attentions" from him. The plural might
be too strong. The singular might suffice.
Hoover had paid attention, objectively and ob-
viously, to her existence.

She was beautiful. She was athletic. She

was scholarly. She explored geological strata.
She could understand what a mining engineer
was doing. Hoover's attention was riveted
upon her. What decision, however, in such a
matter—a matter concerning a young lady
from pleasant home circumstances—could be
reached by a young man transporting ore with
his hands in a mine or riding camels across
the homeless Western Australian desert? But
now! In China, at Tientsin, a home might be
established. So, promptness!

On February 10, 1899, in Monterey, at noon,
Hoover married Lou Henry. At two he took the
train with her to San Francisco. At noon the
next day he sailed with her to China.

China fixed Hoover's success. It made him,
after strange chances soon to be narrated, a
partner in Bewick Moreing and Company, in
1902. It led on to his becoming, in 1908, an
operating and consulting engineer, with a
world-wide practice, on his own account. It
produced no sundering, then or thereafter, of
his links to America.

Business, if nothing else, would have obliged
him to keep his touch with America in the
course of his continuous drawing upon America
for American engineering personnel and for
American machines and materials to be intro-

duced abroad. In every year of the whole of his foreign experience—except in 1898 and in 1907—Hoover spent at least a month (and usually several months) in the United States.

From 1902 forward—while he was still in the midst of his world-travels—his growing reputation as a disseminator of American ideas and things brought him election to membership in a long series of American organizations.

His own technical professional American organizations—such as the American Institute of Mining Engineers, the American Association for the Advancement of Science, the American Society of Civil Engineers, and the Engineers Club of San Francisco—enrolled his name. It was enrolled likewise—during that same period —on the membership lists of the Lawyers Club of New York, the City Club of New York, the University Club of New York, the University Club of San Francisco, the Pacific-Union Club of San Francisco, the Bohemian Club of San Francisco.

In 1909 he became a member of the Republican Club of New York.

In 1912 he was elected a trustee of Stanford University.

These numerous American institutions—it is manifest—did not regard him as an "expatriate."

He was not then in politics; and nobody had yet charged him with having become a "British citizen."

Naturally no document substantiating this charge has ever been produced. It could not be. It does not exist. A search nevertheless was inspired and instituted through the records of the British naturalization authorities in London in order to establish—painstakingly and protractedly—the negative truth. There followed, from the Under Secretary of State in the British Home Office, addressed to Messrs. Broad and Son, solicitors, of London, on March 3, 1920, the following communication:

"I am directed by the Secretary of State for the Home Department to say that no application for naturalization has been received from Mr. Herbert C. Hoover either under the British Nationality and Status of Aliens Act, 1914 and 1918, or under the Act previously in force—the Naturalization Act of 1870."

But Hoover's abstinence from British citizenship—a citizenship which many Americans have found tolerable and convenient and pleasing—was not a fact of mere chance. It was not a mere matter-of-fact fact. It was also an intensely emotional fact.

This tinge in it is described in a communication dispatched to our Government in December

of 1916 by our Ambassador in London, Mr.
Walter Hines Page. Speaking of Mr. Hoover,
Mr. Page then said:

"Hoover was approached on behalf of the
British Government with the suggestion that if
he would become a British subject the Government would be pleased to give him an important
executive post, with the hint that if he succeeded
a title might await him. His answer was:

" 'I'll do what I can for you with pleasure;
but I'll be damned if I'll give up my American
citizenship.' "

Behind the expletive in that answer was the
homing impulse in a man who during all his ad-
ventures abroad had not only kept offices and
club-memberships back in "The States" but
had also, at an immense cost of energy for himself and his family, maintained homes there, inhabited at every fleeting opportunity, in Monterey, in San Francisco, in New York, in Palo
Alto.

As much exportation as possible of American
principles and of American products into foreign lands! As much personal survival as possible out of foreign lands back into America!
That was the mood in which Hoover had traveled. That was the mood in which he looked at
the homeward-bound Americans in London in
August of 1914.

Many of these Americans, he noted, were temporarily in really desperate circumstances. They had funds in America. They had no negotiable funds with them in London. They could not buy accommodations for their return to the United States. In many cases they could not even pay for their accommodations in London hotels and boarding-houses. They were genuinely—for the moment—destitute.

Hoover thereupon took a resolve which changed his whole future. He took a resolve which ultimately was to make him Secretary of Commerce in the American Government and a candidate for the American Presidency. The moment of that resolve, though he did not then at all know it to be so, was the moment when his private career ended and his public career began.

Purely instinctively, out of impulse, out of emotion, with no calculation of consequences, for no consequences were visible, he organized immediately an "American Relief Committee." This Committee, with Hoover as its instantly operating head, proceeded to finance all Americans in London (who could not finance themselves) for their voyage back home across the Atlantic.

Day after day Hoover labored, in the Savoy Hotel, directing questions to Americans and taking their personal paper from them. This paper, with his O. K. upon it, could be cashed at a certain London bank. Hoover—together with associates whom he had inspired to join him in it—guaranteed the bank against loss. Almost any personal paper of almost any American in London became good credit and good money.

Is Hoover possessed of almost fanatical confidence in American character? He has reason. His American Relief Committee in 1914 in London accepted the personal paper of Americans to the value of one and one-half million of dollars; and its losses on bad checks and unkept promises amounted to four hundred dollars in grand final total.

In the course of the Committee's efforts Mrs. Hoover was obliged to leave Mr. Hoover in order to take their two boys—Herbert and Allan —back to school in California at Palo Alto.

The first of those boys, at the time of his birth, had caused Mrs. Hoover much international anxiety. She had formed a fear that if he were born in England he might be by nationality English. She had therefore formed also the design of returning to America to have him born there with no confusing blot upon his American escutcheon. It took legal reports from the American Embassy in London, based upon constitutional researches by the Embassy's lawyers, to reassure her. Even then she insisted upon formally registering both of her boys, not only at the American Embassy but also at the American Consulate, immediately upon their births, as American citizens. Thus certain that they were Americans, from the technical international standpoint, she and Mr. Hoover had proceeded to be also sure that they would be Americans from the standpoint of temperament. To that end they had put them into the public school system of Palo Alto—and were later to put them into Stanford.

Mrs. Hoover, departing from London for Palo Alto in the autumn of 1914, with the children, was to be followed immediately by Hoover himself, who had already engaged his passage.

There arrived, however, in London, from Belgium, a delegation seeking a man. This man was to undertake a task of high diplomacy as well as of high business management. He was to head the effort to persuade the German invaders and the British blockaders to permit the encircled Belgian people to be fed, and then he was to feed them.

In the consummation of an effort so open to the mutual suspicions of the belligerents there was much need of the neutral prestige of the United States. The man desired should therefore undoubtedly be—it was felt—an American citizen.

In the delegation from Belgium, or in co-operation with it, there was an extremely powerful and effective Belgian business man of the name of Francqui. Francqui, it happened, had known Hoover in China. Their purposes there had not always lain parallel. They had indeed crossed and clashed. Nevertheless—and perhaps therefore—Francqui knew Hoover very well.

In our London Embassy our Ambassador Page was resident and observant. He, too, now knew Hoover. He knew him very favorably as the American who had stepped forward to rescue fellow-Americans stranded on the Embassy's front doorsteps.

Francqui said: "The man for Belgium is Hoover."

Page said: "The very man. He has just proved it."

Thus it happened; and thus the relief of Americans sucked Hoover into the relief of Belgians—with consequences how far-reaching and how long-continued!

For eight years, as Chairman of the Commission for the Relief of Belgium, as Food Administrator for the United States Government, as

Executive Officer after the Armistice for the
Supreme Economic Council at Paris, as manager then for the American Relief Administration in Central and Eastern Europe, as
manager thereafter in that same region for the
European Relief Council, and finally as supreme
dictator of the measures for the combating of
the famine in Russia, Hoover was to be incessantly engaged in the provisioning of populations and in the handling of laborious and
intricate negotiations with their governments.

The negotiations were the conditions precedent to the provisioning. The diplomacy had to
come before the food, and then continuously go
along with it.

What preparation either for being a colossal
wholesale grocer, or for being a diplomat, had
ever fallen to the lot of this geologist, this
engineer?

The fact was that Hoover had stopped being
simply an engineer in 1898—three years after
his gaining of his degree at Stanford—while
employed in recovering gold for Bewick Moreing and Company in Australia.

He thereafter was engineer plus superintendent, engineer plus executive, engineer plus
promoter of sales, engineer plus organizer of
credits, engineer plus reorganizer of the

finances of failing companies. In other words,
from 1898 to 1914, on the foundation of his
technical geological and engineering knowledge, he had been increasingly—and, in the
end, primarily—a business man, a man of industry and of commerce.

He became in those years almost everything
in the line of business except a speculator. I
mention that fact neither in praise nor in dis-
praise. The speculator is often one of the most
useful, one of the most impelling, levers of
human practical progress. The stock market,
however, never attracted Hoover. He did not
care much about profits out of the shuffling of
pieces of paper. He was interested in, fascinated by, the exchanges of commodities. He
belongs by nature and by experience thoroughly
to the producing rather than to the banking side
of the business process.

To that producing side, however, he devoted
himself extremely comprehensively from the
very moment when Bewick Moreing and Company, in 1898, enlarged him from being engineer
to being also superintendent and manager.

That promotion was indeed one of the first
points—and one of the most important points—
on which Hoover taught American technique to
his European employers. The European practice was, in each mining enterprise, to have a

technical bureau and a commercial bureau quite separated from each other. The engineers, under this practice, remained engineers only. The commercial managers managed with little engineering understanding or outlook. It was a rigid, a compartmented, system.

Hoover was able to install the contrary American flexible system. He was able to put himself into the business side—as well as into the blueprint side—of Bewick Moreing and Company's Australian enterprises. He thus produced for the company a management combining technical knowledge with commercial touch and reach. He thus produced personally for himself a career in which he was obliged to be not only a student and reporter of geological structures and of veins and seams of ores but also a large-scale handler of organizations of men and a large-scale buyer and seller of almost all known basic commodities.

It was a career which obliged him also, long before he undertook the relief of Belgium, to know and to note the qualities and the contrasts of a score of governments and of swarm after swarm of governmental departmental officials.

That is the point of view from which the private business life of this ultimately public man becomes really genuinely instructive.

Australia: "The most regulated white man's country in the world."

What astonishment and shock for a young American mine-manager accustomed to American conceptions of private property!

Prospectors, as in America. The seeking and staking out of claims, as in America. But the outcome? Not the acquisition of the mines in full private fee simple. Only the acquisition of a sort of leasehold. The title still remains somewhere, somehow, in the Government.

And the leasehold itself remains, moreover, contingent upon use. The mine-manager wishes, let us say, to suspend operations for a while. Enter, at once, a governmental official called a warden. The mine-manager must ask the warden for permission to suspend.

And wages! There is a dispute, let us say, about wage-levels. Or there is a dispute about the "classification" of an employee. Does the work which he is doing entitle him to a higher level or to a lower level of pay? Enter, again, the warden, or a judge, sitting in a court. The Government itself, through one of its branches, the judicial branch, will tell the mine-manager the proper height, or depth, of his wages.

The Government will also build—and operate —every mile of railway bringing in his supplies and taking out his products.

Such spectacles could teach the mine-manager from America much more than he could learn from any Australian engineering problem. For what were the engineering problems?

Was water scarce in the gold-fields of Coolgardie and Kalgoorlie? Was it sold at sixty cents a gallon? Did the wives of mining officials bathe their babies out of a tea-cup of it? Was it found principally in shallow pools, which were salt? Did the salt have to be taken out of it? Very well. Condensers, after all, could work at Coolgardie and Kalgoorlie exactly as well, and upon the same principles, exactly, as at Carson City, Nevada.

And did the water have to be squeezed out of the ore-mud for use again? One of Hoover's American engineering assistants—Frank West —could think of the filter-press used in American sugar mills to squeeze water out of sugar-pulp. It would squeeze under the Southern Cross. The American mine-manager could, and did, bring in—wherever he went—a multitude of American colleagues and a multitude of American contraptions: boilers, dynamos, air-compressors, air-drills, stamp-mills, cyanide plants, pyritic smelters. Around their familiar Americanism a foreign society, nevertheless, still remained foreign, strange, uttering its lessons—or its warnings.

Australian police. Well managed. Very effective. Not much disorderliness. No prohibition agents. No prohibition. Considerable drinking. Considerable gambling. Little murdering. Little stealing. Little actual crime. Police not controlled by the mining-camp. Controlled from a distant capital. Frontier-policing not done by the frontier. Done by the agents of an orderly civilization in the rear.

The American mine-manager could think back to very different scenes in America. A mine of Janin's in New Mexico. A self-governing county. A locally elected sheriff. A town ringing with revolver shots. An old abandoned mine-shaft. A windlass. A bucket. The sheriff hurling his prisoners into the bucket and lowering them, by means of the windlass, to his amateur jail at the bottom of the shaft. Locally influential citizens, deserving the bucket, still at large and still shooting.

Hoover could see governmentalization, centralization, at a high extreme, at an instructive extreme, in Australia. He remained an anti-governmentalist, an anti-centralist. He remained so not on simple theory. He remained so after extended and complicated experience.

It is that experience that gives genuine weight now to his views. The merits of governmentalism and of centralism he has seen; but he has seen also, as he believes, their deadly propagation of creeping paralysis in the initiative and independence and dignity of the individual man.

At the end of the Great War he could say, with a persuasive world-wide observation behind his words:

"The war nationalizations of railways and of shipping are our two greatest problems in governmental control awaiting demobilization. There are many fundamental objections to continuation of these experiments in socialism necessitated by the war. They lie chiefly in their destruction of initiative in our people and the dangers of political domination that can grow from governmental operation.

"The ultimate inefficiency that would arise from the deadening paralysis of bureaucracy has not yet had full opportunity for development, but already we can show that no government under pressure of ever-present political or sectional interests can properly conduct the risks of extension and improvement or be free from local pressure to conduct unwarranted services in industrial enterprise."

Speaking thus strongly against governmental submergence of the individual, he has spoken equally strongly against governmental central

submergence of the local town, county, state.
He has said:

"Through the character of our government
as a confederation of sovereign states, each
with major power and responsibilities for the
welfare of its own citizens, there were established forty-eight experimental laboratories for
development in government. In a sense the
state governments may be called central laboratories themselves; for the illustration may be
carried further, as there are hundreds of little
laboratories in each state. The counties and the
municipalities are also working ceaselessly on
problems of human welfare. They have been
vigorously conducted laboratories. Their experiments have not always been successful; but
the very failures in some states have profited
their sister states, and the injury of failing
experiment has been but local. The successful
experiments have spread from state to state
with constant improvement until many of these
newly invented ideas and institutions have become universal. From their experience our
federal institutions have also benefited.

"A centralized government could never have
taken the risks which many of these experiments
have implied, and under such a government
progress would have been infinitely slower and

perhaps so slow as to have warranted the anticipation of ultimate national disaster which has often been prophesied by our critics. If we can retain our state sense of independence and responsibility in developing our institutions there is, however, no fear of our atrophy. Our real problem is to prevent the surrender of sovereignty by state governments.''

I am well aware that such views are often attributable to the simply selfish desire of a business man to escape strong control over his business by a strong centralized authority. Hoover might be open to this charge of consulting only the interests of the capitalists, of the employers, were it not for the now thoroughly known fact that in the conflict between employers and organized labor he has occupied the position not at all of a partisan but of a neutral judge of the common general public interest. It is not known widely, however, that this willingness of his to meet organized labor halfway goes back to the days when he was himself immersed in personal managerial struggles with employees banded into trade-unions.

His first large-scale contacts with trade-unions were in Australia. He did business in that tightly unionized country in virtually every successive year from 1898 to 1907. He made money in that country for himself and for

his employers and his clients. He never had a
strike there. It is further literally true that in
the course of sixteen years as a manager and
employer—in countries numbering at least
twenty and exhibiting employees who varied all
the way from the highest civilization to the
lowest savagery—he never had a strike anywhere. Yet he could not have allowed his employees to run over him; for he made money and
paid dividends. I shall accordingly now quote
his views on labor, not as they are to-day when
public life may have affected them, but as they
were when he was in the dusty thick of the
employer-employee conflict.

In 1909 he published a volume on ''Principles
of Mining.'' On toward the end of this volume
he discusses ''labor unions.'' The gist of what
he says about them is as follows:

''As corporations have grown, so likewise
have the labor unions. In general, they are normal and proper antidotes for unlimited capital-
istic organization. Labor unions usually pass
through two phases. First, the inertia of the
unorganized labor is too often stirred only by
demagogic means. . . . Lack of balance in the
leaders often makes for injustice in demands.
. . . As time goes on, men become educated in
regard to the rights of their employers. . . .
When this stage arrives, violence disappears

in favor of negotiation on economic principles, and the unions achieve their greatest real gains. Given a union with leaders who can control their members, and who are disposed to approach differences in a business spirit, there are few sounder situations for the employer; because agreements honorably carried out dismiss the constant harassments of possible strikes."

In those remarks by Hoover, the mine-manager, there can be seen indeed the roots of the social views of Hoover the public man. Engaged in commerce, Hoover was never only commercial. He was always almost sentimentally proud of belonging to a "profession"—a "profession" with social duties. In his book on "Principles of Mining" he betrays that feeling in a passage virtually unique among his writings: unique because his own inward emotion in it carries him to the actual touching of outward eloquence. He says:

"There are moral and public obligations upon the profession of the mining engineer. . . . The very essence of the profession is that it calls upon its members to direct men. . . . From the nature of things, metal mines do not, like our cities and settlements, lie in regions covered deep with rich soils. Our mines must be found in the mountains and deserts where rocks are exposed to search. Thus they lie away from the centers of comfort and culture. They are the outposts of civilization. The engineer is an officer on outpost duty, and in these places he is the camp-leader. By his position as a leader in the community he has a chieftainship that carries a responsibility besides mere mine management. His is the responsibility of example in fair dealing and of good government in the community. . . .

"In but few of its greatest works does the personality of the real creator reach the ears of the world. But the engineering profession generally rises yearly in dignity and importance as the rest of the world learns more of where the real brains of industrial progress are. The time will come when people will ask, not who paid for a thing, but who built it.

"To the engineer falls the work of creating from the dry bones of scientific fact the living body of industry. It is he whose intellect and direction bring to the world the comforts and necessaries of daily need. Unlike the doctor, his is not the constant struggle to save the weak. Unlike the soldier, destruction is not his prime function. Unlike the lawyer, quarrels are not his daily bread. What is engineering? Engineering is the profession of creation and of construction, of stimulation of human effort and accomplishment."

With such views—social views—incipiently
public views—Hoover extended out of Australia
to almost every other mining region of the
world (except South America) his grubbing
search for copper, zinc, silver, lead, coal, gold,
graphite, iron, tin.

He is voyaging in the Java Sea, the South
China Sea, the Malacca Strait, the Bay of Ben-
gal. A fellow-passenger tells him of a railroad
he is building in Burma. He says that this railroad goes up into the North Shan states. He
says that near its right-of-way he has stumbled
into some very old abandoned mine-workings.
He says that he has taken out a preliminary
claim upon them from the Government. He
hopes that this preliminary claim will bring him
an exploration title. He thinks that the prospect is all magic—or else all moonshine. He
wishes an engineer could go up there to say
really which.

Hoover gets to Colombo in Ceylon. He presently begins to be possessed, himself, of dreams
about that North Shan state, about that jungle,
about that old mine in it. He picks out a young
engineer from his staff. He dispatches him to
go up the Irrawaddy River and to look.

The young engineer comes back reporting a
glittering possibility of much metal.

Hoover dispatches an older engineer to see if he will catch the same enthusiasm. The older engineer returns with a report of even much more metal—to be got, however, by much sinking of capital and much gathering of labor.

Hoover decides now to go and look himself.

The Burmese rice-fields. The Burmese swamps. Malaria. Fever. Several weeks of bed. Several weeks of delirium. At last, far up the Irrawaddy River, Mandalay. At last, well beyond Mandalay, the North Shan state.

High hills. Thick forests. Little interludes of cleared wet ground and rice. Not far eastward, China. Not far northward, Thibet. A border-land between truly Chinese and truly Burmese populations. A hollow in the jungle. A pit. A pit three hundred feet deep, a thousand feet wide, a half mile long. Marks of the implements of the ancient workmen who dug the pit. Marks of their gradual discouragement about it and ultimate abandonment of it. Marks also, though, of riches, extensive and spacious riches, which their ancient Oriental technique could not solve. The reports of the railroad contractor and of the young engineer and of the older engineer had not been moonshine. Here, awaiting the magic of the technique of the Occident, were zinc, lead, some copper, silver.

But whose were they? All Shan states—

whether called "Northern" or called "Southern"—were "native," yes, but also British. They illustrated the British genius for establishing a régime neither fish nor flesh, but both, with additionally a good red herring drawn across the trail.

The Shan states—Hoover learned—were microscopic but very numerous. The name of this one was Hsipaw. It had a ruler who informed Hoover that his family had sat upon the throne of Hsipaw for eighteen hundred years. This length of lineage, however, he also informed him, involved a certain disadvantage. In the course of it his family had become related, more or less, to most other families in Hsipaw. This gave them a sort of right to visit his palace and eat meals in it. Here was an expense. He had plenty of expense. What he needed more, he felt, was revenue.

His title was that of Sawbwa. He was the Sawbwa of Hsipaw. His personal name was Saw Hke. He had been educated in England in Oxford University. He had twenty-seven wives. One of them was the daughter of the Myosa of Kehsi-Mansam. He had an heir-in-chief named Saw On.

He had some sixty thousand subjects. He had also, dwelling within his kingdom, an immense number of "Nats"—spirits—who constantly intervened in the affairs of his subjects. His subjects had never built a bridge across the neighboring river. The "Nats" had forbidden it. They had let his subjects know that anybody who built a bridge across that river would fall off from it into the fatal torrent beneath.

Hoover negotiated with the Sawbwa. The Sawbwa had power. He had power to collect royalties on all such Shans—subjects of his—as he could persuade to go to work for Hoover. This was a task requiring persuasiveness indeed —and royal inbred tact. Shans are accustomed to living in bamboo huts and wading in paddy-crops. Digging holes into rocks and building bridges condemned beforehand by the "Nats" was not within their calculations. It was necessary to convince them—and therefore necessary also, and first, to convince the Sawbwa.

It was also further necessary, however, to convince the British Lieutenant Governor of Burma and the British "Superintendent" or "Resident" who dwelt near the person of the Sawbwa. Nothing was farther from the intentions of the British than that Shan potentates should give away Shan natural resources gratis to non-Shans.

They had accordingly provided that in the Shan states "the right to all minerals is reserved to Government" and that no foreigner

should be allowed "to take up land as a speculation or otherwise than for bona fide use" and
that "substantial progress shall be made in
applying the land to use" and that a breach
of that engagement would result in an instant
forfeiture of the lease.

Therefore Hoover negotiated with the British authorities as well as with the Sawbwa. He
learned the oldest in Oriental patriarchal government and the newest in modernistic Imperial
Super-Government—charged often with being
predatory, but revealing itself often as being in
fact genuinely and beneficently protective.

He proceeded then—under permits—to develop the Sawbwa's old pit into a new property,
a new community. He crawled with a colleague
into a low long tunnel left by the workmen of
centuries ago. Water filled most of it. Hoover
crawled through the water on his knees and one
hand. In the other hand he held a candle. By
the light of the candle, after a hundred yards or
so of crawling, his colleague stated that he
thought he saw something ahead of them at the
bottom of the water. Hoover looked, and saw
it too. It was the footprint of a tiger; and the
toe-marks of it led inward, onward, in the same
direction in which the explorers were proceed-
ing. They always thereafter laid claim to a
record. It was the record for a hundred-yard

dash, backwards, on two knees and one hand, by candle-light.

To replace that tunnel Hoover built a new one two miles long. It drained the water out of the old pit. He connected the pit by railroad to Mandalay. The new railroad which he built was a hundred miles or so long, under permit from the British Lieutenant Governor of Burma, and it crossed two ranges of mountains and also the river defended by the "Nats."

Hoover imported a young American engineer to build the bridge. This boy constructed the span of the bridge on one side of the river and then pushed the span across the river till it found lodgment on the other side. He then started walking across on a girder. In the middle of the span the "Nats" got him. He fell off and dropped fifty feet into whirling water. He was swept downstream.

Presently, however, the spirit of America met and fought the spirits of Hsipaw. The young American engineer struggled. He flung himself toward shore. He was hauled out exclaiming "Nats."

With the railroad came workers, non-Shan as well as Shan. Many were Chinese. They had no objection to any kind of work. The Shans themselves were tempted to work by a new phenomenon: ready cash money. Soon, close by

the old pit, there was a new community with
twenty-five thousand inhabitants. They spoke,
by groups, some seventeen different languages.
In intercourse between groups they spoke principally some few words of Pidgin English.

The Sawbwa was glad enough to see them.
He taxed them, and he also administered justice
among them—subject, however, to the British
provision that his punishments should be "in
accordance with good conscience and in con-
formity with the spirit of the law in force in the
rest of British India."

Thus alien brutality or beneficence thrust itself into the Hsipaw idyll. Land tenure in Hsipaw was especially idyllic. It nourished the
ideal of community control. It discouraged individual tenaciousness. The occupier of land
held it only as from the treasury of the community and only as trustee. He could not sell
it. He could not mortgage it. His children
could not of right claim it. He might in the
course of any year see it transferred to some
neighbor thought more worthy. An annual distribution of lands was effected at the will of an
official called a "Nebaing." He represented the
common welfare against personal possessive-
ness.

How beautiful! How beautiful in principle!
In practice how ineffective! At the end of cen-

turies of communal agriculture the Shans in
Hsipaw had reduced to cultivation only about
two per cent. of the country's area!

Hoover shipped silver and zinc and lead in
large quantities out of Hsipaw. He shipped
lead-pig out of Hsipaw to be smelted in the
United States. He imported new artifices into
Hsipaw and exported out of it old refuse turned
by him into new value. He took away—for himself—within himself—some little new additional
knowledge of the infinite variety of social institutions and of governmental manners and
methods among men.

Similar increments of such knowledge came
to him—bit by bit—as he observed New Zealand, even more "advanced" than Australia;
Japan, most effective of all Oriental lands in
resistance to foreign armed might; Korea,
classic proof of the proposition that national
inoffensiveness does not necessarily mean national security; the Malay States, essential to
Britain if she would properly protect Australia
and New Zealand; Ceylon, essential to Britain
if she would properly protect the Malay States;
Egypt, essential to Britain if she would properly protect Ceylon; the Transvaal and Rhodesia, essential to Britain if she would properly
protect the Cape of Good Hope and maintain a

second route to the Orient in the potential default of Egypt; India, exhibiting supine political lethargy in its native-ruled states and exhibiting democratic political awakenment really only in such of its states as have fully and directly experienced the so-called "oppressions" of the British!

Social weakness inviting conquest and Empire!

Empire spreading schools and laws and social strength.

Social strength then repulsing Empire!

All this pageant of the politics of the Orient was for Hoover, as he negotiated with government after government under Asiatic and African skies, a penetrating and impressive education in political science; and he needed it.

In his school-boy and college-man days he had not dug truly to any deep distance into the political strata of the past. He had not nourished himself—in the manner of William Edgar Borah or James A. Reed—on the debates in the American Constitutional Convention of 1787. He had not nourished himself—in the manner of James Madison and of the other principal framers of our Constitution and founders of our country—on the political debates and governmental altercations of Rome, of Athens, of all time. He had not gained from books what now he was obliged to gain—inch by inch—from the rubbing of his geological and commercial nose against irremovable walls of political and governmental dominant fact.

He could begin to see now that government is the canopy that protects all human life from the winds of chaos and that politics, which provides to that canopy whatever supports it may have, is in truth man's central structural activity.

In this matter he was again, indeed, "lucky." If he had stayed in the United States, where government is stable, and where its stability is inhaled by engineers and by business men with as little gratitude as they give to the air, he might have gone on for many years a thoroughly non-political person. His travels forced him—literally and lavishly forced him—to realize that stable government is not manna from heaven but human heroic aspiration rooted in slime and blood and reared to success only by sacrifice—and then vigilance.

One more of his belated lessons may here be briefly recited. China!

The Gulf of Pechihli. The Port of Taku. The River Pei. On its banks, toward Peking, Tientsin. An office there for Hoover, in 1899, as Engineer-in-Chief of the Chinese Imperial

Bureau of Mines. A house, a home, for his bride.

There and then began the almost preposterous passion of Mr. and Mrs. Herbert Hoover for opening and closing houses. The shortness of their sojourn in almost any given spot seemed seldom to discourage them from opening a house. They were to open one in Sydney and in Kalgoorlie and in Melbourne, Australia; in Petrograd and in Kyshtym, Russia; in Mandalay, Burma; and in numerous other foreign towns. In the course of their globe-trotting years they were to open seven houses in the United States, in California and in New York. The mind faints at contemplation of the hours that Mrs. Hoover must have spent opening and closing houses, renting houses, packing.

From Tientsin, though, she migrated with her husband on many miles of exploration for mines that would be useful to the ambitions of China and to the ambitions also of Chang Yen Mao, Chinese Imperial Director General of Mines, mandarin politically, plutocrat personally.

Exploration by caravan, by cavalcade, in pomp. Number One Topside Foreign Devil Chief Engineer Man—that is, Hoover—could not be permitted to travel without pomp, without face.

Saddle horses. Mules. Ponies. Carts. Sedan-chairs. Grooms. Footmen. Cooks. Valets. Cot-beds. Charcoal-stoves. Pots and pans. Ambulating kitchens. "Hoover man so expensive China cannot let die for small things."

No mining code. Will Hoover compose mining code? He will. At night-time, after the Number One Boy and the Number Two Boy and all the rest of the servants have served the evening meal, Hoover reads Chinese history, Chinese metallurgy, Chinese law.

He has always been a night-time reader. He will sleep till two and then wander about the house—or tent—and read till four, or so, and then resume sleeping. He keeps long business hours. He thereupon reads nocturnally.

He seems to need little sleep—and less exercise. He also eats with the rapidity of a farm-hand. He is temperate in the amount he eats but rather intemperate in the speed with which he eats it. His inherited wholesome and hearty constitution, fortified by his outdoor toils in his youth on farm and in desert and on mountain-range, seem to enable him with impunity to defy the preceptors of protracted chewing and of daily golf. He is due nevertheless, if he should ever become President, to have to listen to many severe professional lectures on the use of the teeth and the legs from his official presidential medical aide.

Out of his night-time researches in China he derived a really considerable familiarity with the history of Chinese governmental civilization. He stitched this knowledge back to his recollections of the mining codes of Australia and the mining codes of the United States. He wrote—as his first effort at legislation—in his twenty-sixth year—a mining code for China.

The adoption of it—and the utilization of his detours and discoveries in Manchuria and Mongolia—were interrupted, however, with a definitive sharpness by the outbreak of the Boxer convulsion.

Mobs. Chinese soldiery joining the mobs. Tientsin beseiged. Mrs. Hoover—as well as Hoover himself—day after day under fire from a Chinese army venting upon foreigners a perhaps understandable hatred with a physical marksmanship highly inefficient and with a political purpose condemned by vagueness to be dissipated presently into empty vapor.

Sympathetically, but scientifically, Hoover could contrast this Chinese ungoverned promiscuous effusion of futile blood with the sternly organized governmental effectiveness which had bloodlessly expelled the Occidental foreigners from all special privileges in Japan.

In besieged Tientsin he learned also his first lesson in what was to be—afterwards—during so many years—his chief public occupation. He became—in an impromptu amateur way—Tientsin's provisioner, rationer, food-controller.

Food was the prosaic basis of Tientsin's deliverance. Hoover operated it. Whatever there has been of the dramatic in his life has been the dramatizing of prose.

He slew no mandarin. He did save one's life.

His Chinese chief—Chang Yen Mao—residing in Tientsin—got badly misunderstood by the local authorities. He was on his way to summary elimination when Hoover intervened —successfully—with a guarantee of his innocence. Thence came many consequences, lasting even till now.

Chang Yen Mao, in 1900, feared for his private properties. Governmental conditions in China threatened them with danger and—possibly—destruction. Hoover joined with other foreigners to extricate Chang Yen Mao from that difficulty by re-organizing his properties —based on mines—into a British-flag concern with a considerably Chinese management enjoying foreign protection but at the same time safeguarding the Chinese interest.

Negotiations to this end were lengthened and roughened by the incapacity of some of the Chi-

nese to stay tied by their own commitments.
Land-titles in China are—or were—unregis-
tered documents, "bearer" documents, documents conveying rights to the possessor with
little or no recourse to any court, even if any
court could be found to take jurisdiction. Certain of Chang Yen Mao's officials attempted to
make sales of title-deeds on Chang Yen Mao's
properties to outsiders while simultaneously
those properties were supposed to have passed
into the control of the newly formed partly foreign and partly Chinese enterprise. Words
high and hot were uttered by Hoover. An
American subordinate of his proceeded to illus-
trate frontier justice in a frontier situation by
seizing physically a considerable number of
documents which Chang Yen Mao's Chinese
staff was selling in the market for its own sur-
reptitious private profit. These incidents—and
certain succeeding ones—have ever since served
to encircle the inscrutable brow of Chang Yen
Mao with a halo as that of a Confucian saint
harassed and harried by Foreign Devil exploiters. The truth is that Chang Yen Mao
saved his financial neck (and perhaps his physical neck) only because of Foreign Devil justice.

Hoover went to London with a report on
Chang Yen Mao's properties. He returned with

capital for their development and became their
manager. They were situated largely in the
Province of Chihli, to the northeastward from
Tientsin, in the neighborhood of Tongshan.
They consisted principally of mines of coal.

Hoover presently, on these properties, had
twenty thousand employees. He built much
railway line. He built a cement works. He did
the first building of the new great harbor of
Chinwangtao. He engaged heavily in the handling of ocean steamers. The new company—
the Chinese Engineering and Mining Company
—became very prominent in China but also
very prominent in financial circles in Europe.

Certain European interests thereupon bought
into it and established a new financial control of
it, with two results.

One: Hoover resigned from his position as
manager. Two: Chang Yen Mao was ousted
from his honorific and lucrative holdings in the
directorate.

Chang's loss of fortune was important
enough but his loss of face was more important
still. He seems to have been visited by his Government with political degradation and he
seems indeed to have been well put on his way
by his Government toward physical execution.

In these circumstances he did an extraordinarily wise thing. He refrained from seeking

justice in the courts of China. He sought justice in London.

He arrived in London, among the Foreign Devils, among the exploiters, to charge certain of them with attempting to cheat him at a spot in an alien jurisdiction on the other side of the globe.

A British judge heard him. He heard him assert that his position in the management of the Chinese Engineering and Mining Company was guaranteed to him by a certain memorandum which he held to be a contract. Witnesses were summoned.

Among the witnesses was Hoover. He testified that he had signed the document. He testified that in his judgment the document was a binding bargain.

All the testimony of the whole case may be readily found in the files of the London *Times* for the early months of 1905.

The net upshot of the exploitation of Chang Yen Mao by Occidental financial imperialists was thereupon as follows:

An American "exploiter"—Hoover—who had already rescued him once from catastrophe —swore that his rights under the memorandum in question had been wrongfully taken away from him. A British "imperialistic" judge—in a merciless excoriation of the wrong—restored his rights to him in full.

He returned to China to be permitted to remain alive and to be permitted to remain rich. He subsequently entrusted Hoover with the disposition of important valuables of his in London.

Chinese character enlarged Hoover's knowledge of men, and Chinese government enlarged greatly his appreciation of the influence of governmental institutions upon men's characters and capacities. He had separated himself from the Chinese Engineering and Mining Company before the wrong upon Chang was committed. He did not return to China. His new fortunes —by the time Chang visited London—had already taken him into the one genuinely distinctive aspect of his business career, an aspect deserving mention for its bearing upon the public duties to which he was presently to be summoned.

We have observed that the mine that Hoover developed in the Shan state of Hsipaw in Upper Burma was a mine already once used. Hoover became a great repairer and restorer and reviver of used mines, a resuscitator of asphyxiated mining companies.

He became—long before he was Secretary of Commerce—a great specialist in the turning of wastes into profits, of abandoned materials into dividends, of lost motions into savings.

It was in his character—or in his fate—that he never did discover and develop any colossal pure lode of precious metal, or solid bed of diamonds, to provide his engineers and workmen with sensations of easy luxury and to provide the stock market with ecstasies and thrills.

No! He had to go and find some vast dump, some horrid heap of once-used black earth, some mountain of "tailings," of rejected refuse from some dead or dying foregone adventure; and then, by preference, or perversity, or destiny, he would find in these discarded cards of those who had sat in the game before him not gold or platinum but some drab base metal like lead or zinc.

He returned to Australia where, in his first youth, he had indeed sought and got gold. Now, however, he went to another part of Australia on another—quite another—sort of quest.

His gold he had got in Western Australia. He now went into Australia's southeastern region, into New South Wales, to a place appropriately and dismally entitled Broken Hill.

Broken Hill was broke. Its chief scenery was millions of tons of earth turned up to the sky—

in a dump—with all their silver and their lead
extracted and gone. Each ton was suspected,
to be sure, of containing zinc; but nobody
seemed to know how to get the zinc economically out.

In the mine itself there remained certainly an
enormous mass of ''proved'' bodies of ore. In
that ore were particles of silver and of lead—
and also of zinc. Without some new and better
method of rescuing and selling the zinc it would
be idle and profitless to disturb the lead and the
silver. The proposition was one of low-grade
material—and high-grade salvage.

Hoover was a salvager of metals in distress
long before he was a salvager of victims of
famine and flood. Most of his life seems to
have been spent salvaging.

He salvaged a million tons of zinc out of the
dump at Broken Hill and he restored the mine
itself there to renewed commercial activity. A
settlement of fifteen or twenty thousand people
had been about to die. Hoover made it live
again. He gave it another existence and another prolonged prosperity.

Such operations required two certain qualities in high abundance.

In the first place, they required a mind imagi-
natively open to new processes which could replace the old ones that were no longer capable

of making the properties pay. In the second
place, they required a large-scale mind, a mind
with a grasp on quantity and on distance, a
mind comprehending not only the getting of the
metal but the carrying of it by rail and by ship
and the selling of it across continents and across
far oceans.

Hoover's business—at its peak—essentially
was to revive a dead mine not only by better
engineering technique but by better and more
spacious commercial marketing practice.

His great effort at Kyshtym in Russia was in
precisely that category. The mining-plant
there had been worked for two hundred years.
The stock of the company owning it had been
bought and sold for a long time in the financial
circles of Western Europe. The romance of
what Hoover did was not the romance of un-
covering a scene unknown in the past. It was
—in a way—the even more creative romance of
quickening a past which otherwise would have
been unknown to the future.

The Romanoffs who owned the plant lived in
circumstances half of the Orient and half of
feudalism. They had hordes of tenants not
far removed from being serfs. They had workmen not far removed from being as antique in
their mental attitude as the mining plant was

in its equipment. Hoover had the task of modernizing not only a plant but a working-force.

He brought in pyritic smelting as pursued and perfected at Butte. He dared to introduce furnaces which would treat thousands of tons a day in place of hundreds. He distilled wood to furnish charcoal. He made and sold by-products from that distillation. He made and sold by-products from his sulphur-gases. How different is this scene from the one in which Hoover is in popular thought shown, traversing the world armed only with a pick and engaged simply and easily and happily—and with no public educative consequences whatsoever—in tapping out gold-nuggets.

Governments, officials, masses of materials, masses of men, land transportation problems, ocean transportation problems; financing problems, selling problems, all on a scale measured by the diameter of the earth: that was Hoover's actual experience in every year of his arrived engineering life.

In the fall of 1913 he took that experience back to California and established himself and his family at Stanford and extended his practice of his profession in the western part of the United States and began to look forward to basing himself less and less on his offices in New York and in foreign lands and more and more on his office in San Francisco.

His new duties as a trustee of Stanford University attracted him. The advancing education of his boys drew him back to the scenes of his own education. He had done engineering in Canada, in Mexico, in many of our states in the Rockies and on the Slope. He had never coveted a fortune beyond a competence. He was possessed now of more than a competence. By the standards of his boyhood he was extremely rich. He has departed singularly little in any way from those standards. He is singularly and almost exorbitantly tenacious of his own traditions. Born in plain circumstances, he has never desired glittering circumstances; and even his wealth in the bank has always been subdued to plainness in his living. By the fall of 1913 and the spring of 1914 his wealth sufficed him for all the plain living that even a highly extended maturity and old age could cause to stretch out before him; and he flattered himself with the prospect of semi-activity in western American business and semi-retirement on the Stanford campus.

Again chance balked him. Again "luck" blew him to another flight in career.

The San Franciscans who were interested in the Panama-Pacific Exposition observed him to be at home. They reflected that he was well acquainted with foreign parts. They reflected that exhibits from foreign parts were decidedly necessary to their expository success. They requested Hoover to proceed back to Europe on their behalf to interest European governments in the coming grandeur of the world-spectacle at the Golden Gate.

Hoover accepted the mission; and Mrs. Hoover packed once more, and once more unpacked in "The Red House," London. The Hoovers had never owned it, but they always kept it on lease as a sort of domestic hotel not only for themselves but for almost all other American engineering London transients; and there they were again!

Speculation! If Hoover had not been willing to undertake the mission to Europe for the Panama-Pacific Exposition, and if accordingly he had not been in London when the Great War broke out, who would have organized the American Relief Committee in London and who would have been called to feed Belgium and who would have become American Food Administrator under Wilson and American Secretary of Commerce under Harding? Not Hoover.

Hoover owes every last tinge of color in his whole present rainbow of fame to his willingness in 1914 to do a chore for San Francisco and California.

It was thus that one day in the fall of 1914 he happened to be sitting with Ambassador Page and some others in the American Embassy in London, discussing Belgium, discussing starvation, discussing who should take charge of Belgium's rescue. He himself had been already much mentioned for that task. He lay between two compulsions.

On the one hand, his wealth had been much shaken by the commercial and financial dislocations produced by the war. Simultaneously the war offered him new wealth in the handling and straightening of those dislocations for himself and for others. The Ambassador knew that an important industrial organization had offered Hoover a hundred thousand dollars a year for his services "to start with."

On the other hand, there was in him a compulsion of which I have yet spoken little and of which I here give just one illustration. When, upon his graduation from Stanford, he was working with his hands at day-wages in the Mayflower Mine, there were boys at Stanford—solid, hard, deserving boys—who in their pockets had loans out of his savings to help them on with their studies.

He did not need, in 1914, to improvise pity and helpfulness. He needed only to act upon them.

Page turned to him at last and said definitively:

"Hoover, you're *it*."

Hoover got up and left the room.

He knew the slowness of governments. He knew the quickness of markets. He had bought and carried food for scores of mining-camps in distant and diffcult spots. He had fed Tientsin. He had fed many hundreds of thousands of people since. Here was a job, however, which would mean the feeding of millions. He left Page and the others and went away for a while by himself.

When he returned Page said:

"Well, what's your answer?"

The answer was one which marked again the quality I have frequently mentioned as the prime spring of Hoover's success.

The answer was:

"I noticed there was an hour more before the exchanges would close in New York. I've bought a few million bushels of wheat for the Belgians."

Who would pay for those few million bushels of wheat? Hoover did not know. He had bought them solely and sheerly on his own responsibility and with the backing only of his own fortune—what there was left of it.

Promptness! And the nerve to take a chance!

CHAPTER THREE

AMERICAN NEGOTIATOR

HOOVER's relief of Belgium was from the beginning an American participation in international diplomacy. It demanded, on Hoover's part, from the beginning, the highest possible qualities as an international diplomatic negotiator.

I shall pass over, with scant notice, his sentiments of kindliness toward suffering Belgians and his feats of spacious efficiency as a wholesale buyer, a wholesale transporter, and a wholesale distributor of foodstuffs. In a longer treatise it might be possible to do justice to those aspects of the matter. Here we are shortly and compactly considering the education of a private character for public governmental opportunity and office. Kindliness is not a sufficient title to kingship, whether in a monarchy or in a democracy. Olympian wholesale grocering is not a final ticket of admission to the company either of Cæsar or of Lincoln.

To be able to feed Belgium, to begin to be able to feed Belgium, Hoover needed capacity not only commercial but in the most ultimate de-

gree political. His past experiences now really
primarily useful to him were not those in mines
but those in the ante-rooms of governments.

It was for Hoover now, in 1914 and 1915, to
construct—almost—and in a sort—a government of his own.

It was for him to construct an institution
which would exchange understandings and
guarantees with the government at London,
which would perform fiscal governmental duties at Brussels, which would sign—in effect—
protocols and treaties with the government at
Berlin, and which would find and maintain its
own fleet of ships flying its own flag: a triangle
of white, emblazoned with the red initials
C. R. B., which gave to the Commission for the
Relief of Belgium a supposed sanctity as of the
Red Cross and at the same time an actual status
as of a new and strange nationality.

Hoover's very first task was to be sure that
this new and strange nationality could actually
financially exist. Private charity could not
alone, by any possibility, sustain it. It is sometimes thought in the United States that Hoover
in Belgium was only Santa Claus handing to
Belgian children the unending offerings of
American charity. The actuality was very different. Charity provided to Belgium in the
course of the whole of its agony only a few tens

of millions of dollars. The total financial income and outgo of the Commission for the Relief of Belgium amounted to many hundreds of
millions of dollars. The overwhelming bulk of
the Commission's financial resources came from
governmental treasuries.

The two blades of the scissors holding the
Belgians helpless in the face of an approaching
country-wide famine were the invading Germans and the blockading British. The Germans
could not well see why they should not add all
Belgium's resources to their own in what they
regarded as a struggle for the security of the
German name and race. The British could not
well see why they should allow Hoover to put
resources into Belgium to be added to the German store and to be added, thus, to what they
regarded as an engine for the subjugation of
mankind.

On September 17, 1914, however, the German
Imperial Governor-General of Belgium, Field
Marshal von der Goltz, informed our American
Minister Whitlock at Brussels that the German
Imperial Government was willing to agree ''not
to requisition the shipments of wheat and flour
destined for the alimentation of the Belgian
civilian population.'' He thus initiated the
guarantees from the invaders; and thereupon

Hoover proceeded to try to wring subsidies from the blockaders.

On November 5, 1914, he sought and gained an interview with Sir Edward Grey, British Minister for Foreign Affairs, and pleaded his case with him. Sir Edward in return accused the Germans of continuing to make requisitions upon Belgian native food-supply. He said that this course of conduct on the part of the Germans "made it very difficult for the British to take a favorable view of themselves contributing money, as this was in effect supplying food to the German army."

The farthest Sir Edward would go was to countenance the grant to Hoover of some five hundred thousand dollars as an experimental British move. There he stopped. He had reason. It was for Hoover to produce from the Germans a series of guarantees that would be more stringent, more efficacious.

Seeking them, and seeking also certain arrangements regarding banking and currency and international money-exchanges in Belgium, Hoover repaired to Berlin.

He held conversations with Zimmermann, the German Under-Secretary for Foreign Affairs; with Helfferich, the German Minister for Finance; with Melchior, the Financial Adviser to the Minister for Finance; with von Jagow, the German Minister for Foreign Affairs; with von Bethmann-Hollweg, German Imperial Chancellor — all within the space of three prompt days. He returned with guarantees and arrangements superior to those which he had previously held from the Germans but still requiring, for their successful application, the loyal support of the German military and political staffs in Belgium itself.

The acquiring and maintaining of that support was most naturally a matter of ceaseless concern and of ceaseless effort. The Germans most naturally did not relish the spectacle of better and cheaper food in Belgium than in Germany. They also feared espionage in Belgium by Hoover's English-speaking subordinates. They even charged some of them— specifically but wholly wrongly—with having committed that crime. They ordered the total number of English-speaking relief workers in Belgium to be reduced to twenty-five. They demanded difficult—and, indeed, impossible—bail-bonds on the canal-boats suffered to ply between Holland and Belgium.

These interferences—inevitable but, if continued, fatal—had to be met by Hoover sometimes with diplomatic tact and sometimes by a method which, in its place, is equally diplomatic: namely, frank firmness.

On February 12, 1915, Hoover outrightly wrote to the German Governor-General of Belgium—now von Bissing—to say:

"Although I feel deeply the responsibility, I am compelled to assure Your Excellency that unless we can establish a basis of confidential and friendly relations and trust from the German authorities, we shall be compelled to withdraw, and the flow of the stream of the foodstuffs into Belgium from outside countries must necessarily cease. We feel that while our service is personally beneficial to the Belgian civil population it is nevertheless of the utmost importance to the Germans from every point of view."

Such negotiations brought ultimately to Hoover a fair and clear field for his distribution of alien food to the populations of Belgium and of occupied Northern France.

There remained, however, always, the necessity of finding the money for the purchase of that food. At one moment—on March 18, 1915 —Hoover was obliged to inform Whitlock at Brussels that the Commission for the Relief of Belgium was now more than seven million dollars in debt. He added: "I do not object to taking this personal liability on myself; but, if I cannot meet it, it simply means that the food supply in Belgium will cease."

Necessity is therefore the quite right word for the force that impelled Hoover to make a frontal verbal attack upon the British Chancellor of the Exchequer, the guardian of the British Treasury.

The Chancellor at that time was Mr. David Lloyd George. In him Hoover encountered as supple, as flexible, as adroit, a diplomat as the war produced. The interview between the two men was in a large degree determinative of the war-time fate of Belgium. Hoover made a memorandum of it from which, for its high historical importance, I quote the pivotal points in full:

"I, to-day, had a meeting with Mr. Lloyd George, at which there were present Lord Emmott, Lord Eustace Percy, and later on Sir John Simon.

"The occasion of the meeting was the discussion of the question of the exchange of money with Belgium.

"Mr. Lloyd George stated that he had put his veto upon the project. It was certainly assisting the enemy. We were giving the Belgians more food resources with which to stand requisitions in food by the Germans. We were relieving the Germans from the necessity of feeding the civilian population of Belgium. We were directly prolonging the war.

"He expressed the belief that the Germans, in the last resort, would provision the people of Belgium. He was wholly opposed to our operations, benevolent and humane as they were, and therefore he could not see his way to grant our request.

"I pointed out that the Germans had given an undertaking that after the first of the succeeding month no requisitions would be made. I read out to him the undertaking which had been given to the American Minister in Berlin. I informed him that we were satisfied that the Germans were carrying this out with the utmost scrupulousness. I informed him that the Germans had impressed none of our actual food. I stated that there was no danger of the Germans taking the money which we collected from the sale of foodstuffs because that money was in the possession of the American Minister at Brussels.

"As to whether the Germans would ultimately provision the civilian population, I told him that I was satisfied that they would not. I recited to him the confirmation by the German military authorities of the current statement in Germany that there was no clause in the Hague Convention obliging the Germans to provision the civilian population of Belgium. On the contrary, it incidentally provided that the civilian populations should support the military.

"I told him, further, that the Germans contended that in taking the port of Antwerp and opening it to neutral ships, they had given the Belgian civilian population a means of provisioning themselves but that this inlet to Belgium had been blocked by the British navy and that the British therefore, according to the Germans, must bear the responsibility.

"I pointed out that starvation had actually occurred in Belgium. I further pointed out the position of the French people in the Meuse Valley. They had not had our assistance and they were dying of starvation under German occupation.

"Mr. Lloyd George denounced the whole of this as a monstrous attitude.

"I replied that—be that as it might be—one matter stood out in my mind. The English people had undertaken this war for the avowed purpose of protecting the existence of small nations and for the avowed purpose of guaranteeing to the world the continuance of democracy as against autocracy in government. It would be an empty victory, I said, if one of the most democratic of the world's races should be extinguished in the process. I said that the English people were great enough to disregard the doubtful military value of advantages in favor of assurances that these people should survive. I said I felt the obligation went further than mere acquiescence in our work. It extended an opportunity to the English to add to their laurels by showing magnanimity toward these people—a magnanimity which would outlast all the bitterness of the war.

"Abruptly Mr. Lloyd George stated to his colleagues:

" 'I am convinced. You have my permission. I would be obliged if you gentlemen would settle the details of the machinery necessary to carry this out.'

"Then, turning to me, he said that I would forgive him for running away but that he felt the world would yet be indebted to the American people for the most magnanimous action which neutrality had yet given way to."

That "I am convinced" by Lloyd George was indubitably Hoover's greatest triumph in the feeding of Belgium. It made the feeding of Belgium possible. Without the political diplomatic persuasiveness and skill which brought Lloyd George to saying "I am convinced," all Hoover's humanitarianism and efficiency and physical instant energy would have been futile.

And for seven years thereafter it was only

continued success as a diplomat that enabled Hoover to continue to be in Europe the most successful relief administrator in that continent's history.

From the British Treasury, on behalf of Belgium, Hoover managed to get some one hundred million dollars during the period between the date of the invasion of Belgium and the date of the entrance of the United States into the war. From the French Treasury, on behalf of Belgium and also (and more particularly) on behalf of occupied Northern France, Hoover managed to get—during that same period— some two hundred million dollars.

The French Government steadily claimed, however, that it was for the Germans to feed the French population in occupied France. It steadily declined to assume any legal responsibility for the feeding of that population. Hoover thereupon spent many hours of earnest expostulation and of ardent exhortation in Paris. He there at length seemed defeated and yet was victorious. The Government had rejected his arguments and requests. He sat in his hotel, desponding. There came to his room a distinguished French banker.

This banker said that he had heard of Hoover's negotiations with the Government and that he personally was extremely interested and impressed. He thereupon went away.

A day or two later to Hoover in London there came a massive amount of francs in a check drawn against a French private banking institution. This check was followed by other similar checks. Hoover applied them instantly without question to his Belgian relief operations.

He was by this time quite accustomed to getting enormous amounts of money consigned simply to him personally or to "Mr. Hoover's Fund." He had been gifted with the foresight, at the very beginning of the whole affair, to employ a firm of eminent and irreproachable accountants to check every item of income and outgo on the books of the Commission for the Relief of Belgium and on his own books. The published reports of those accountants gave to all contributors, whether governmental or private, a completely detailed statement of every phase of Hoover's Relief stewardship.

They incidentally revealed a fact which was not so much creditable to Hoover as discreditable to the people who were surprised by it. They showed that Hoover had naturally refrained from paying himself any salary out of the funds of the Commission for the Relief of Belgium and had also refrained from causing those funds to bear the burden of a pound or a penny of the whole cost of his incessant and extremely extensive Belgian Relief travels. He had worked, and he had traveled, for Belgian Relief, at his own cost, wholly.

It may here properly be added that in the business world in which Hoover used to move it is thoroughly known that not since the time when the Great War cracked the foundations of his fortune has he ever had the chance to repair them. He was due to come to the moment when his salary as Secretary of Commerce would be a welcome addition to his annual income.

Sympathy, indeed, is not thus necessitated for him. No public man who has become relatively poor requires sympathy when a return by him to private life would almost instantly restore him to immense wealth. The only appropriate comment upon such a situation is that here is a man for whom a prolonged abstinence from immense wealth is no deprivation in comparison with the loss which he would have felt if he had been deprived of the opportunity for public effort.

The French private checks that Hoover received in London in 1915 he turned into the treasury of the Commission for the Relief of Belgium with a sense only of puzzled gratitude.

The checks were so large that they seemed to
represent a private beneficence of almost incredible proportions. Not for several months
did Hoover divine the truth about them. The
truth was this:

The French Government was determined to
maintain the fiction of its complete legal irre-
sponsibility for the relief of the French population in occupied Northern France. It nevertheless could not bear to see that population
perish. It accordingly was sending French
public money to Hoover under cover of French
private names.

With that discovery Hoover felt assured of
continued and competent French and British
financial public backing in Belgium.

He had not hesitated, however, to solidify
his prospects of getting that backing by issuing
his first international diplomatic public note.
It was an appeal to the people of the United
States.

The Commission for the Relief of Belgium
had been permitted by the British to undertake
its labors in Belgium on the express understanding that all its shipments of food would be
consigned to the American Minister at Brussels. The American Minister at Brussels, the
American Minister at The Hague, and the
American Ambassador at London had become

honorary presidents of the Commission for the Relief of Belgium. They had given the Commission their personal public approval and—with the sanction of the State Department and of the White House—they had given it the moral authority of the Government of the United States.

Hoover seized upon that international diplomatic fact. He forged out of it a friendly weapon against doubts and delays at London and at Paris. At a moment when those doubts and delays were threatening the dissolution of his whole activity in Belgium, he went right over the heads of London and of Paris and appealed directly to the national sentiments of his own fellow-countrymen. He most audaciously—but absolutely successfully—announced:

"The Commission for the Relief of Belgium takes the gloomiest possible view of the future. . . .

"It is desirable that the American people should understand why both sides in this gigantic struggle have refused to accept the responsibility for the feeding of these people.

"The Germans state that by throwing the harbor of Antwerp open to neutral trade they have been acquitted of the responsibility; because nothing prevents the normal flow of trade into Antwerp except the Allied navy. . . .

"The English and French affirm that they cannot allow free trade with Antwerp; for there can be no assurance that the enemy will not be supplied thereby. . . .

"The logical consummation of these views could only mean the decimation of ten million people. . . .

"An accommodation must be found quickly. The world's greatest tragedy looms larger and larger. . . .

"The English and French should give us financial support to feed their allies. The Germans should cease to reduce—through levies and requisitions—the ability of these imprisoned people to help themselves. . . .

"If all fails, the neutral world and future generations will lay the responsibility for the decimation of these people at the proper door, and no mixture of military reason and diplomatic excuse will cloud the issue. . . .

"The magnificent generosity of the American people, which has proved neutrality no barren negation, will have been wasted unless each of these belligerent peoples comes to its rightful share in saving from starvation these millions of men, innocent women, and children. . . .

"We have stated our case bluntly and frankly. Our only court of appeal is American public opinion; and it is for America to say whether a crime shall be committed which will bring this generation down in infamy to posterity.''

The effect of this utterance was momentous. American opinion was solidified into regarding Belgian Relief not only as an American charity but as an American national public policy. Hoover thereafter, as Chairman of the Commission for the Relief of Belgium, became in full effect the American governor of an international state protected physically by the Germans, supported financially by the British and the French but maintained politically by the American people.

This extraordinary governmental international institution—the product of an emotion but the product also of a laborious and intricate and daring diplomacy—Hoover was now able to reduce to routine.

In Rotterdam, in Holland, docks, ships. Some eighty ocean-going tramps, tramping from Australia, from Argentina, from Manchuria, from the United States, flying for protection against submarines the triangular red-lettered C. R. B. flag.

A flow into Rotterdam of some four hundred million pounds of C. R. B. foodstuffs a month.

Canals. Five hundred canal-boats. Thirty-five tugs. By water, still, these foodstuffs proceed into Belgium.

In Belgium some forty Americans—only, at the most, forty—volunteers—supervising the reception of these foodstuffs, supervising their distribution.

Distribution effected into every commune in Belgium and in occupied Northern France. Five thousand communes. In all of them, warehouses, soup-kitchens.

Forty thousand Belgian and ten thousand French assistant-distributors.

Presently two million three hundred thousand children eating a special C. R. B. meal every noon-time.

A population of ten million buying its food, or getting it gratis, from one foreign middleman, who is watched for all possible un-neutral conduct, daily and hourly, by German inquisitors and by Allied spies.

Tins of condensed milk. The C. R. B. serves the milk and leaves the tins. The Germans pick up the tins and carry them to Germany. Lord Eustace Percy, of the British Foreign Office, very properly takes notice. He orders Hoover either to bring the tins back from Belgium or else quit sending condensed milk in.

The Germans drive some cattle into Belgium to graze. Lord Eustace tells Hoover that he must cease importing into Belgium any more fodder-maize.

Lord Eustace discovers in Brussels a flour-miller named Vyulsteke who is receiving C. R. B. grain, pressing it for its oil, and then selling the oil to Germany for use in munitions. Hoover must stop Vyulsteke.

The Germans annoy Lord Eustace in other particulars and he naturally writes to Hoover to say:

"I now must ask you to stop all shipments into Belgium of soap, coffee, sugar, oleomargarine materials, yeast materials, butter, salt, groceries, cheese, dried fruits and vegetables."

Fast trips by Hoover to Berlin. Tedious talks with high German dignitaries. Concessions.

Fast trips by Hoover to London. Forty voyages by him, backwards and forwards, in the midst of submarines and torpedoes, across the English Channel. Tedious talks with high British dignitaries. Concessions.

In the end, all formalities of examination waived for Hoover at all ports, at all frontiers, from France to Britain, from Britain to Holland, from Holland to Belgium, from Belgium to Germany. He becomes the world's one accepted automatic neutral. His baggage passes unopened. His person passes unsearched. He earns this exemption by his thoughtful habit of tearing up all pieces of informative paper and of remembering nothing military.

In the end, a half of the population of Belgium and of Northern France obliged to seek food gratis.

In the end an expenditure, by the Commission for the Relief of Belgium, for supplies, of approximately one billion dollars.

"Overhead" administrative cost, on the buying and distributing of these supplies: less than one-half cent per dollar.

Surely as much experience in the management of food for famine as could appropriately be offered to, or imposed upon, one man.

Yet, just as Hoover's large-scale handling of materials in his mining business was merely a preparation for his larger-scale handling of materials in Belgium, so his experience in Belgium turned out to be only a preparation for another subsequent similar experience—similar but larger scale still.

In the middle of the year 1917, the United States having declared war upon Germany, Hoover's troubles in Europe were interrupted, and he embarked upon some new troubles— politically—as United States Food Administrator at Washington.

His successes as Food Administrator—and, interwoven with them, his first struggles with the domestic political consequences of scientific administrative measures—may logically be deferred for consideration to the moment when it will be in order to relate his similar successes and struggles as United States Secretary of Commerce.

It will at this point be more convenient in thought and more intelligible in narrative to resume and to conclude the tale of the labors awaiting him still on the eastern side of the Atlantic Ocean, and now not only in Belgium but in virtually the whole of Europe.

On October 21, 1918, Hoover conveyed to President Wilson a comprehensive memorandum outlining the methods that could and should be employed to rehabilitate Belgium immediately upon the signing of the Armistice.

It is to be noted, then, that Hoover's return to Europe in the fall of 1918 was accompanied by a first thought for the resumption of an old duty. New duties, nevertheless, and larger ones, were now to claim almost all of his European time.

These new and larger duties were pressed upon him by two sets of combining circumstances.

Before him lay, in Europe, in the enemy countries and in the countries about to be liberated from the enemy countries, vast populations long deprived of adequate sustenance and now in large part on the very verge of starvation.

Behind him lay, in the United States, vast supplies of food built up by the price-promises made to the farmers of the country by the Congress and by the President and by the Food Administration authorities.

Hoover perceived the desirability—the necessity—of bringing the European needs and the American supplies quickly together.

On Armistice Day—again that promptness! —he handed to President Wilson a program directed to this end. It had been approved by the War Department and by the Shipping Board. It directed the War Department to purchase within twenty days two hundred and forty million pounds of flour and some thirty or forty million pounds of pork. It directed the Shipping Board to carry those materials at the earliest possible moment to French ports. There they would be reconsigned by Hoover "to the territories lately held by the Central Empires."

Hoover imagined that he thus had contrived both the provisioning of liberated Europe and the utilizing of the surplus food produced by

American agriculture under war-time stimulants.

He sailed for Europe on the fifth day after the Armistice, as Director of Relief.

He was walking into what might paradoxically be called a nightmare of awakenment.

He had expected that the Allied Governments would recognize in peace-time the understandings which they had reached with him in wartime. Nobody had thought that war-time would end so soon. The Allied Governments had laid out a buying program for themselves, extending far into the year 1919. Hoover, to meet that program, to coöperate with the Allies in the winning of the war, had laid out a corresponding producing program for the farmers of the United States. He had permitted himself to expect that since we, as producers, had fulfilled our program, the Allied Governments, as buyers, would fulfill theirs.

He learned better fast. The Allied Governments could now buy food cheaper elsewhere than in the United States. On December 31, 1918, the Allied Meats and Fats Executive in London announced that it was inexpedient to place further orders for pork in the United States. Simultaneously each of the three Allied Governments announced the complete can-

cellation of their entire pork orders in the
United States for the month of January. These
orders had totaled some three hundred and
sixty million pounds.

Ten days previously Hoover had received
from the Chief of the Food Administration's
Meat Division in Washington the following
cablegram:

"We must have orders for four hundred million pounds of pork for January and the same
for February, or disaster will follow."

That cablegram was temperate. The United
States was indeed producing a surplus of four
hundred million pounds of pork a month, and
it was producing it under a price-agreement
which, if shattered by loss of markets, would
plunge a large section of our agriculture and a
large section of our industry and commerce into
a country-wide panic.

Our farmers had produced hogs on an undertaking that the average price-level of hogs
would be $17.50 a hundred pounds. Our pack-
ers had produced pork from hogs which they
had taken at that level. Our stockyards were
full of high-priced hogs. The run of hogs to
market in December of 1918 and in January
and February of 1919 was turning out to be by
a great margin the largest on record. Our
warehouses were full of high-priced pork and

were getting to be—if one may so put it—fuller every hour.

This pork was not indestructible. It was perishable. It had to be sold within a reasonable time. Also, it had to be sold at a reasonable price. It had to be sold at a price bearing some relation to the high price at which the raw material for it had been bought. Otherwise two results would follow.

One. Our packing industry would be bankrupted.

Two. Our packers would cease to buy hogs; and the stream of hogs now flowing to the stockyards would be turned back upon the farms; and the 1917-18 crop of hogs, instead of bringing a promised prosperity to our farmers, would bring them collapse and ruin.

Hoover was now in a most singular situation. He was not only the world's foremost large-scale humanitarian but also the world's foremost large-scale pork salesman and history's greatest international drummer for bacon and lard.

He had stationed himself at Paris. Though he was not accompanied by Mrs. Hoover, he had established himself in a house—on the rue de Luebeck—which became transient headquarters for all Americans effectively interested in European relief from starvation and prostration.

He had seen three possible sets of customers for his pork.

The first set would be the Allied Governments. The second set would be the Central Powers. The third set would be the peoples liberated from the Central Powers: the Poles, the Czecho-Slovaks, the Jugo-Slavs, the Roumanians, and so on.

Now the Allied Meats and Fats Executive had checked him in the Allied direction.

He had already turned in anticipation and with energy to the next most vital direction: Germany. He had suggested to the assembling authorities of the Peace Conference that the Allied Governments should now permit a free and open trade with "the neutrals"—that is, with Holland and Norway and Sweden and Denmark—and that "the neutrals" should thereupon be allowed to exchange commodities with Germany, giving food in return for manufactures. Thus the people of Germany might again be able to have a diet capable of preserving them from disease and death.

This suggestion drove toward economic sense as much as toward humanitarian decency. It was unhorsed. It was ditched. On December 31, 1918—on the very same day on which the Allied Meats and Fats Executive decided to stop buying pork from the United States—the

Allied Blockade Council made a decision even more crushing. It decided that "the neutrals" could not be allowed to provision Germany. It decided that German women and children, as well as men, must continue to be under-nourished, malnourished, subjected to increasing sickness and to a mounting death rate.

Turned back thus from the portals of Germany, as well as from the entrances to the Allied markets, Hoover was reduced to his last hope: the liberated peoples. He labored at this hope with some success but also with much repeated failure. He discovered soon that the feeding of the liberated peoples was hinged not only on ethics and on economics but also on politics—the politics of a continent long necessarily unaccustomed to the speeding of any international arrow unfeathered by political calculations.

Hoover approached distraction and despair. He came closer to them at this instant than at any other in his whole career. He was tormented by the spectacle of a coming physical breakdown—and chaos—in Central Europe. He was tormented by the spectacle of a coming economic breakdown—and wreckage—in the United States. He could see perfectly clearly the thing which, by linking the two breakdowns, could prevent both. It was—grotesquely enough—ridiculously enough—the American hog.

Humanitarianism, prosperity, civilization, seemed to rest for the moment on a foundation of snorts and squeals, of corn-cribs and swill-pails. Hoover in his youth—like many other people—had taught himself to seek sleep by imagining a stile and by imagining sheep leaping it and by counting them as they went over. He found that now, as he lay on his bed, these sheep had been replaced by pigs. He would lie —night after night—counting a pig, a pig, a pig, a pig, a pig, a pig, a pig.

Four hundred million pounds of them a month! To be sold somewhere! Somehow!

Nor were these pigs, as a matter of fact, by any means the whole of the burden on Hoover's mind. As Food Administrator for the United States, as Director of Relief for Europe, he had ordered many things besides pigs to be shipped to European ports to await there his further orders. His promptness, his willingness to take chances, which so often had made him great, seemed likely now to lay him flat, to destroy him, to bury him in a failure as deep as his previous successes had been high. He at one certain moment during this period in Paris had more than one-half of a billion of dollars' worth of American foodstuffs piled up skyward on wharves in European ports—with no purchaser of it permitted and no consuming destination of it allowed.

His delirium and his indignation he proceeded now to visit upon the innocent—and almost equally indignant—heads of President Wilson and of the other members of the American Peace Delegation.

Hoover's letters of this period are the severest indictments of Europe ever written by an American.

On February 4, 1919, he wrote to President Wilson, and sent him three resolutions which he thought should be passed by the Supreme War Council, and said:

"These resolutions have three main purposes.

"First. There is no right in the law of God or man that we should longer continue to starve neutrals, now that we have a surplus of food.

"Second. The French, by obstruction of every financial measure that we can propose for the feeding of Germany, and in the attempt to compel us to loan money to Germany for this purpose, have defeated every step so far suggested for getting them the food which we have been promising for three months. The object of the second part of the first resolution and of the second resolution is at least to find some channel by which the Germans can help themselves by trade with neutrals and South America.

"Third. The object of the third resolution is to allow the people bordering on the Mediterranean to get into production and trade with all their might and, by so doing, not only revive their commercial life but also to a large degree supply themselves with food.

"I have worked consistently since arriving in Europe on the twenty-fifth day of November to secure these objects and I have to confess that although they have been accepted in principle in one department and in one government after another, they are constantly defeated by one bureaucratic and special self-interest after another in the various governments; and I can assure you that the blockade against neutrals and the Southwest of Europe is being used to-day for purely selfish ends, when its sole justification was for the furtherance of military operations, which justification is now gone."

Two weeks later, on February 19, 1919, Hoover wrote to the American Peace Delegation as follows:

"Up to date not a single pound of food has been delivered to Germany. It will be recollected that the German mercantile shipping was taken over from them on a positive assurance that Germany should have food. It is a bargain upon which the United States is on record, and it is unfulfilled.

"The old blockade, under which the neutral countries of Europe are half starved, is still enforced, except for some minor relaxations, and this despite the continuous efforts made by American officials since the Armistice. First one excuse and then another have been found by one government after another among the Allies for refusal to relax this blockade. . . . The uses to which the blockade on foodstuffs is being put are absolutely immoral. They are entirely foreign to the whole purpose of the war and I do not feel that we can with any sense of national honor or dignity longer continue to endure this situation.

"I have by consent and approval of the Allied Governments been set up on behalf of the United States as the central figure engaged upon the food supply of Europe as a whole, including the amelioration of food conditions to neutrals, relief to the liberated countries, and supply to enemy countries. I have as yet accomplished nothing except in so far as I have been able to directly draw upon the United States resources, which I have poured in to the last penny of our ability. I wish to solemnly warn the Conference as to impending results in the total collapse of the social system in Europe unless this matter is at once straightened out."

Such were Hoover's feelings at Paris toward the European situation and toward the governmental factors in it. He arrived, in the midst of those feelings, at two ultimate views which would seem—to me, at any rate—to be highly contradictory.

He counseled an adherence by the United States to the League of Nations. He simultaneously counseled—with a wisdom and an authority certainly much more directly based upon his own experience in his own special field of action—a withdrawal by the United States from all coöperation in European collective economic alliances and entanglements.

He became the most conspicuous specimen of that peculiar and almost incredible hybrid: an international political Wilsonian under the same hat with an international economic "Irreconcilable."

I must at this point state an extremely unimportant fact. I must state it in order that the reader may realize that at this point I am not writing about Hoover with objective detachment. The unimportant fact in question is that in 1919 and 1920—because of Hoover's advocacy of American participation in the League of

Nations—I regarded him with precisely the same feelings which I might have entertained toward anybody who was trying to steal George Washington out of his tomb in Mt. Vernon and scatter his ashes upon the waters of the Potomac; and I still think of the League of Nations precisely what I thought then. I think that an American signature to the League of Nations would be a thorough mis-reading of this country's origin and nature and a profoundly dangerous mis-directing of the natural and proper development and destiny both of this country and of Europe.

I am unable, accordingly, at this point and in this matter, to be very much impressed by Hoover's idealism. I am much more impressed by what I conceive to have been his error. Idealism does not extinguish error. It merely moralizes its momentum and multiplies its menace.

I perceive, of course, the influences that impelled Hoover toward his League-of-Nations position.

A Quaker by blood and a humanitarian by habit, he has both an inherited and an ingrained predisposition toward peace. He thereupon has also an inevitable impulse toward at least a friendly examination of any apparatus declared by its inventors to be a preservative of peace.

Hoover's hatred of war is not like that of many of the sudden pro-Leaguers of 1919 and 1920 who, from desiring the blood of every German baby, turned in the twinkling of an eye to shuddering at the thought that any Serbian should ever henceforward be permitted to bayonet any Macedonian brigand.

Hoover's love of peace is no compensatory reaction from a despicable and degraded blood-thirstiness. It is a love of peace which embraced a willingness to allow the German nation to survive defeat, just as it had previously embraced a determination that defeat should not annihilate the nation called Belgian. It is a love of peace which is not soured even by war. It is a love of peace which—in a word—has really something to do with love.

I take it that every lover of peace who deserves any genuine moral respect must have demonstrated a little interest not only in safety but in human lovingkindness. Hoover has most certainly done so. He has done so—and does so—not only in his works of mercy but in his inward temperament as evidenced by his daily intercourse with persons who are not at all the objects of his works of mercy. He is exceptionally devoid—in ordinary business moments as well as in high humanitarian emergencies— of the poisons of personal hatreds. Resentments he feels—and angers—in response to aggressions; but the envy and the malice that produce or accompany aggressions are almost entirely alien to him. Within the limitations which must be put upon any such assertion regarding any sinful human worm, it can be said with an approximate approach to a tolerable accuracy that Hoover does not hate.

At the same time, I cannot call him, entirely, a "pacifist." That word has come to cover a field broader than Hoover can or does fill. Hoover does not show any tendency to commit suicide if the navy gets another cruiser. He does not brandish and bray a vast vocabulary of "war-lords," "imperialists," "militarists," and "minions of the munitions-makers." His idealism does not cause him to bury his realism beyond resuscitation. He does not propose to arrive at peace by taking two inches off the length of bayonets or by directing personal vituperations at social cataclysms.

Most emphatically, he is not a peace-mono-maniac. Most emphatically, nevertheless, he is indeed a man about whom it is necessary frankly to say that in him there lies an abiding streak of the philanthropic mysticism which never has been more memorably expressed than in our own days by the Irish poet George Russell in the liquid lines:

"Lights of infinite pity star the gray dusk of
   days.
Surely here is soul. With it we have eternal
   breath.
In the fire of love we live, or pass by many
   ways,
By unnumbered ways of dream, to death."

With Hoover, by religion, in principle, hate is
death; and life should be love; and love, of
course, should be peace; and so there you are!
It is mental attitude rather than a policy. A
mental attitude, however, it most certainly is;
and it most certainly had much to do with enabling Hoover, in the very thick of all his economic pre-occupations, with barrels of flour and
crates of potatoes and cargoes of hogs, to see in
the League of Nations whatever of good could
be brought to visibility in it.

In the second place, Hoover was bound to
be influenced—without perhaps any consciousness of it at all—by his loyalty to the man who
was then his chief. Wilson had trusted him.
He trusted Wilson. He had experienced not
only Wilson's charm—which was virtually in-
vincible for those upon whom he chose to exercise it—but also Wilson's undeviating confidence.

To be sure, he earned that confidence. He

earns it still. A multitude of Wilson's inti-
mates have written books and articles from
which Wilson emerges with slivers under his
fingernails and with his brains alleged to have
been provided to him by the auditors of his
soliloquies and by the couriers of his battle-
plans. To such disparagements of the mighty
man whose purposes had no colleagues, and
whose policies had only pawns, Hoover has contributed not one book, not one article, not one
word.

Because of Wilson and because of the League
of Nations Hoover vibrated and vacillated in
1920 between being a Republican and being a
Democrat. It was an unquiet and inconsistent
interlude in his life. It bore an appearance of
"independence." It was occasioned in large
part by a quite different quality. Hoover's un-
derlying and abiding nature is better revealed
by the combination of his loyalty to Wilson then
and his applauded—and excoriated—loyalty to
Coolidge now.

Hoover is, in truth, and at bottom, not an
"independent" or "mugwump" at all but intensely an "organization man." In institutions of which he may be the head he expects
faithfulness. In institutions of which he may
be a member he renders faithfulness. Like
every really great organizer, he is himself

capable of being organized. Like every really great commander, he is himself a "good soldier." Let it be called a virtue. Let it be called a vice. It is a fact.

I would not be thought to mean for a moment that Hoover in 1919 said to himself:

"I am against the League; but Wilson is for it; and I also will therefore be for it."

That would be preposterous. I have already mentioned the reasons why it would be preposterous. Hoover was a sort of natural Native Son for the New Jerusalem sub-division of Geneva. I only mean that when he saw his trusted chief, Woodrow Wilson, about to assault the political battlements of Europe and about to plant upon the apex of the European donjon-keep the conquering and liberating flag of all humanity, he was perhaps as much taken by the valor of the crusader, who had already led him to so many victories against evil and wrong, as he was by the validity of the crusade, to which he certainly had not yet given much specialized thought.

The League of Nations was, and is, necessarily an adventure in politics. It comes out of governments, and it goes back to governments; and they consult, necessarily, both their own politics and the politics of the international arena. I have already drawn attention to the absence in Hoover of any youthful passion for political studies. I have drawn attention to the fact that his knowledge of governments came to him only gradually in the course of his dealings with them as mining engineer, as business man, as economic departmental public administrator. He had been successful in those dealings. He had learned much. He was now intimately familiar with governments in their administrative aspects. He had dealt little with them, however, in their popular political aspects. He now, with this preparation, at Paris in 1919, faced two challenges.

The first was the proposition—the League of Nations proposition—that there should be established in Europe, with American participation, an international *political* collectivity.

The second—equally strenuously advocated by the Europeans—was that there should be established in Europe, with American participation, a corresponding international *economic* collectivity.

We would pool our political endeavors, against war and for peace; and, correspondingly, we would pool our bread-and-butter endeavors, our natural resources, our basic products, our distributions and enjoyments of the fruits of the earth.

Each proposition was in principle as fraternal, as noble, as the other. To the political one Hoover, the economist, said "yes." To the economic one Hoover, the economist, said emphatically and totally "no."

He continuously maintained—in numerous conversations with Mr. David Lloyd George in the Peace Conference period—that all the economic "pools" which had been created internationally during the War should forthwith now be dissolved. Now each country should resume its management of its own economic affairs. Now each country should give back to private traders their responsibilities and their opportunities in the management and furtherance of trade.

"A wound," said Hoover repeatedly to Lloyd George, "is cured in the end only by the wholesome action of the cells. In this world-wide wound give the cells a chance."

Moreover, in the course of following this line of thought and in the course of observing the actual daily behavior of European governments in their relations with him as Director General of Relief and as Chairman of the Supreme Economic Council, Hoover began to draw back from many—even—of the political coöperations proposed in the Treaty of Versailles.

He wrote, on April 11, 1919, to President Wilson, a letter never surpassed for its portrayal of the dangers of American participation in European internal conflicts and adjustments. This letter, saturated as it is with a belief in the League of Nations, may be filed in the library of any "Irreconcilable" as a classic analysis of the European conditions and tendencies which ultimately sent the United States back to its old policy of intervening abroad only on supreme occasion and not by daily rote.

Nothing else that has ever come from Hoover's pen is so fundamental as a public document or so valuable as a searchlight upon the gradual groping growth of his international political thought. I shall therefore quote from it all its main observations and conclusions.

"Dear Mr. President:

"Your economic group has had before it the question of whether the United States should continue membership in the various commissions set up under the Peace Treaty. . . .

"I feel strongly that any continuation of the United States in these commissions can only lead to vast difficulty. . . .

"First. Our presence on these commissions would appear to be for one of the following purposes:

"A. To give moral and political support to the Allied Governments in measures generally for their benefit. In this event the United States will be lending itself to the political and financial interests of other governments during peace—a situation that must be entirely repulsive to our national interests, traditions, and ideals.

"B. Another objective might be that we should remain in these commissions with a view to securing justice and moderation in the demands of the Allies against the Central Empires. We would thus be thrust into the repulsive position of the defender of our late enemy. Our experience during the last three months has shown us bitterly that we thus subject ourselves to complaint and attack from the Allied Governments, and such a continued relationship could only breed the most acute international friction.

"Second. The continuation of such a relationship will bind us for a long period of years to a succession of compromises fundamentally at variance with our national convictions. One other practical result of our experience already is that the Americans who sit on such European commissions, if they do not acquiesce and assist in enforcing any propositions from various governments, become immediately and personally subject to attack as being inimical to their interests. These governments, if they were faced with the sole responsibility for their actions, would not attempt the measures which they seek under our protection.

"Therefore I do not see that we can effect any real justice in these matters.

"Third. If we continue to sit in the enforcement of this peace we will be in effect participating in an armed alliance in Europe. We will be obliged to participate in all European questions.

"Fourth. This whole matter has a very practical relationship to the League of Nations. If we can bring to an early end our whole relationship to these political combinations in Europe, which grew up before and during the war, and can lend our strength to the League of Nations, that body will gain in stability and importance which it could not otherwise attain. If we can again secure our independence, we can make of the League a strong and independent court of appeal that will have authority.

"Fifth. I am convinced that there has grown up since the Armistice the policy—perhaps unconscious, but nevertheless effective—of dragging the United States into every political and economic question in Europe and constantly endeavoring to secure pledges of economic and political support from us in return for our agreeing to matters which we consider for their common good, where we have no interest, and constantly using us as a stalking horse, economically and politically, solely in the interests of internal political groups within the governments. These objectives and interests may be perfectly justified from their point of view but it forces us into violations of our every instinct and into situations that our own people will never stand. For instance, I do not see how we can remain in these enforcement commissions, unless we participate in the military enforcement, with its enormous cost and risk; and the tendency here will be always to exact the political objectives, with the military strength of the United States as a background.

"Sixth. I have no doubt that if we could undertake to police the world, and have the wisdom of statesmanship to see its gradual social evolution, we would be making a great contribution to civilization; but I am certain that the American people are not prepared for any such measure; and I am also sure that if we remain in Europe with military force, we shall be forced into a storm of repression of revolution and forced into it under terms of co-ordination with other peoples which will make our independence of action wholly impossible.

"Seventh. It grows upon me daily that the United States is the one great moral reserve in the world to-day and that we cannot maintain that independence of action through which this reserve is to be maintained if we allow ourselves to be dragged into detailed European entanglements. In my view, if the Allies cannot be brought to adopt peace on the basis of the fourteen points, we should retire from Europe, lock, stock and barrel. If they cannot be brought to accept peace on this basis, our national honor is at stake and we should make peace independently and retire. I know of nothing, in letter or spirit, of any statement of your own, or in the fourteen points, that directly or indirectly ties the United States to carry on this war through the phase of the enforcement of the multitudinous demands and intrigues of a great number of other governments and their officials. It does appear to me that your conception of the League of Nations was with a view to the provision of a dominant court, where these difficulties could be thrashed out. If we sit as one of the prosecutors, the court will have no judge.

"Faithfully yours,
"HERBERT HOOVER."

In comment upon this letter—so down-on-the-ground in its view of the actual nature of Europe—and so soaring in its view of the supposed nature of a coming League of Nations—there are three main observations that are bound to occur to any serious and diligent inquirer into the development and expansion of Hoover's political philosophy.

In the first place, it is manifest that a pursuit of world-peace—through a League—had temporarily drawn Hoover away from his normal political moorings.

Hoover was a Republican by birth, by upbringing, by deliberate affiliation. His only membership in any political club was in the Republican Club of New York City. In 1912—in the course of the triangular contest between Wilson and Taft and Roosevelt—Hoover's farthest thought away from Republicanism was in the direction of a profoundly moved interest in the Republican "Progressivism" of Roosevelt.

Then came, however, that lofty vision—or, if one so pleases to regard it, that celestial will-o'-the-wisp—that drew so many eminent Americans across so many marshes of disappointment: American alleged leadership in world-peace-settlement.

It was for this that Hoover counseled his fellow-countrymen in the fall of 1918 to rally behind the President and to give him a Senate and a House of Representatives politically loyal to him in order that in the approaching Peace Conference he might speak to the world with a politically coherent United States behind him.

It was for this that in 1920 he for a moment played the rôle of a political neophyte who would enter either the Republican or the Democratic convent if only the habit it would wear would be the habit of an Americanized world-peace system.

It was for this—later on in 1920—when his natively clinging Republicanism had again reasserted itself—that he joined thirty other magnificently distinguished and magnificently deluded Republicans in issuing a manifesto to the American people declaring that the best and shortest road to the palace of peace at Geneva was through a White House inhabited by Warren Gamaliel Harding.

They were deluded because Harding at that very moment was irrevocably personally pledged against ever actually taking the United States into the League organism.

It is to be noted, of course, that the Republican company in which Hoover thus found himself was spacious as well as exalted.

Among the forty-nine Republicans in the United States Senate there were only fourteen who were wholly anti-league. All the rest—including Harding—voted for the Covenant with reservations.

Senator Watson of Indiana so voted. Sena-

tor Curtis of Kansas so voted. When Hoover
said, "I stand for the League with the Republican reservations," he was on the same side
with the superficial votes—though not on the
same side with the subterranean sentiments—
of the Republican senatorial majority.

He was on the same side with ex-Governor
Lowden of Illinois who said: "I believe in the
passage of the League of Nations Covenant
with reservations."

He was on the same side also with Calvin
Coolidge who said: "If the security of Europe
is so intertwined with the League of Nations
that we can make the best progress by taking
the good in the Covenant and by amending
those things which are not consonant with
American traditions, surely the Republican
platform permits of such a course."

He was on the same side also with Charles
Evans Hughes and Elihu Root who joined him
in assuring the electorate of the United States
that with Harding as President it would soon
be elevated to the sublime task of pacifying
mankind.

This cloud of highly placed co-witnesses does
not diminish or dull, however, the fact that
Hoover witnessed to a millennium that never
happened; and, accordingly, having noted that
the beauty of that millennium was a high mo-

tive of his politics in 1919 and 1920, we may
pass on to trying to find out precisely where
for him its beauty lay.

We have observed that Hoover, in his letter
of April 11, 1919, to President Wilson in Paris,
wanted the United States to refrain from becoming a party to any of the commissions and
quarrels under the Treaty of Versailles because
those quarrels would go to the League as to a
court and because then, in the League, "if we
sit as one of the prosecutors, the court will
have no judge."

It is manifest therefore that Hoover shared
a view which was widely current among pro-
League Americans.   It is manifest that the
League of Nations which he had in mind was
a most extraordinary League in which the
United States would never be prosecutor, never
be culprit, never be plaintiff, never be defend-
ant, never be a participant in a dispute, never
be a partisan to a cause, but always be serenely
and securely and only the ultimate judge.

In other words—to put it brutally—Hoover
was for a League which was a fadeless amaran-
thine floral tribute to his conception of the
status of the United States in the world but
which Europe—having, after all, its own history and its own destiny and its own pride—
could never in practice accept.

The European rejection of our reservations to our adherence to the League of Nations Permanent Court of International Justice is now proof positive of this proposition. The continent of our origin is never going to purchase peace at the price of becoming a political suburb of the District of Columbia.

It is scant wonder that as the actual living League of Nations has more and more unfolded its natural and inevitable pre-occupation with European control of European fate, the distance between Washington and Geneva has apparently seemed to Hoover to be longer and longer and more and more paved with thorns.

He thought he could take American control to Europe. He simply has found out that it cannnot be done.

We may thereupon note the third and final conclusion that his League-of-Nations letter to President Wilson suggests. That letter is as ingrowingly an American document as exists in American political literature. For what does it preach?

Europe is sunk in its sins. The sole savior in sight is the land of the free and the home of the brave. The free and the brave, however, must be careful not to get too deep into the European hell-hole. They must save it, as it were, from its brink. They must, as it were, remember that "he who sups with the devil needs a long spoon." "Fellow-citizens," the document seems to proclaim, "rescue these perishing people but, for Heaven's sake, don't get to be like them."

I distrusted Hoover the pro-Leaguer; but, "Irreconcilable" as I am, I could never get to be quite so super-American as that!

Hoover, however, in Paris, in the early part of 1919, had still on his mind the powerful lesson taught him by those hogs—those American hogs—slaughtered so trustingly in defense of civilization for our noble Allies and now, as pork, so callously not wanted by them.

A few concluding words must here accordingly be given to Hoover's final flight through the European sky as a salesman of pork and as a deliverer of Central and Eastern Europe from the most imminent famines of modern times.

That pork did, after all, get sold. The populations of Central and Eastern Europe did, after all, get fed. The price-level of hogs for the American farmer did, after all, get maintained till the 1917-18 harvest of hogs, started and finished under the encouragement of the price-promises of Hoover's Food Administration, had been marketed.

Hoover kept the export-surplus of hog-products flowing out of the United States, and he kept it filling up his temporary reservoirs on wharves in European ports. He caused his Food Administration Grain Corporation to become the transitory buyer and holder of a lot of it. He caused his Commission for the Relief of Belgium similarly to become the transitory buyer and holder of a lot of it. He then drummed and drummed—in the most incessant and insistent American commercial-traveler style—till he persuaded the French and Italian Governments to reinstate with him a considerable proportion of their canceled hog-products orders. He battered and battered at the walls which the Allied Supreme Military Command and numerous Allied commercial interests still maintained between him and the Central and Eastern European mouths and markets. He thrust as much food as he could through all the chinks and slits in those walls. Finally, in March of 1919, a frontal attack upon them by American and British forces in combination threw a long sector of them down flat, and Hoover's food was given permission to begin to penetrate even Germany.

On March 26, 1919, the first German payment for supplies from America was deposited in Belgium. Hoover was so prompt this time

that he had his first food-ship for Germany—
the *West Colfax*—unloading at Hamburg the
day before.

The rest is a tale of statistics drying up tears
—and so not so dry.

When Hoover's food-ships would tie up at
northern European ports, and cargoes of flour
would be trundled across wharves into warehouses, women and children would come and
scrape up leavings of flour with dust off the
wharves and carry the dirty mixture off in
handkerchiefs or eat it then and there.

As this is a book about Hoover, we will not
dwell on the suffering seen or on the pageantry
of the pity felt. We will dwell on the works
necessitated.

There came into existence, by Hoover's need
and requirement, the American Relief Administration. It was at first a public arm of the
United States Government, supplementing the
United States Food Administration and the
United States Food Administration Grain Corporation and handling—among other great resources—the one hundred million dollars ap-
propriated by Congress for relief in Europe to
hungry people whose hunger was not German
or Austrian or Hungarian "enemy" hunger.

Later the American Relief Administration

was transformed by Hoover into a private organization linked in practice to the European Relief Council which was promoted by Hoover in the United States for the raising of thirty-five million dollars of private American money for the relief of European suffering in general.

With such backing the American Relief Administration proceeded to make virtually all Europe between the Rhine and the Urals into its parish.

It distributed food in sixteen countries.

It sold food for currency. It delivered food in return for obligations of foreign governments sent back into the United States Treasury. It gave food away.

It at one moment was serving meals to four million children daily.

In Poland alone it had fourteen regional warehouses, one hundred and twenty district warehouses, seven thousand six hundred and fifty feeding centers, and—at the peak of its work—one million three hundred thousand children gathered into those centers for their daily meals.

In 1922 Antoni Ponikowski, President of the Cabinet Ministers of Poland, announcing the formal termination of the work of the American Relief Administration in Poland, dispatched to the world the statement:

"This work has meant health and life to over one and a half million of Polish children. It has preserved a generation for Poland. The entire population of Poland worships the name of Hoover."

By that time the famine in Russia had summoned the American Relief Administration to a field even more extended both for horror and for help.

Thirty-five thousand feeding stations were necessary in Russia. The number of men and women and children fed daily mounted to a peak of eleven million.

Part of the money for this service was furnished by the American Congress. Part of it was drawn from a renewed outburst of generous American private charity. Some twelve million dollars in gold was negotiated by Hoover out of the coffers of the Russian Soviet Government.

Hoover tolerated no defeats in Russia for his representatives by the diplomacy of the Soviet Government. He got the Soviet Government to contribute to his purposes, and then he kept the management of those purposes in his own hands. He stretched a cordon of three hundred reliable American volunteers across Russia from the mouth of the Neva to the mouth of the Volga. He built up in Russia

an organization of one hundred and twenty-five
thousand Russian assistants responsive to his
policies. His chief American representative,
Colonel William N. Haskell, was able to report,
at the end of his labors, in 1923, that:

"We demonstrated, above all, that at least
one organization could in Russia exist and succeed without submission to dictation."

Hoover had begun his experiences as an
American negotiator in Europe with a successful siege of the diplomacy of London. He
ended them with a successful siege of the diplomacy of Moscow. In the interim his name
had become—next to that of Wilson—the best-
known American name in Europe.

A rain of ribbons and buttons descended upon
him. He put up a firm and thick umbrella
against them. One decoration—just one—from
France—did break through. So did one title.

The Belgian Government summoned him to
La Panne. It lay in the little slice of Belgium
never conquered by the Germans. The Belgian
King and the Belgian Queen were there. The
members of the Belgian Cabinet were there.
The war was well over. The moment for rewards had arrived. The Belgian Government
was confronted with a puzzle. It was Hoover's
detestation of decorations. It had been solved.

A decoration had been contrived which was not a decoration because it carried no ribbon or button; and it was not an order because nobody else would ever belong to it. After a little lunch in the little royal cottage the Belgian King and Queen and the Belgian Cabinet made Hoover—without precedent and without succession—"Citizen of the Belgian Nation and Friend of the Belgian People."

When he first got back from Europe after our entrance into the Great War and was about to become United States Food Administrator, at the end of so many years of foreign wanderings, and after so much residence in London, I noticed a very tiny thing.

I had known many Americans who had lived long in London. I had seldom or never noticed this thing in one of them before.

It gave me my first impression of the almost combative inward resistance that Hoover has to outward environment.

He had not accumulated one smallest touch of that most contagious of all foreign social products: the English accent.

He spoke an American as uncontaminated by London refinements as if he had never left Iowa.

This imperviousness of his—thus tinily illus·

trated—is both to the bad and for the good. It keeps him lonely. It kept him American.

As Food Administrator he was now about to begin—tardily—but with an American heart and mind—the last lap of his protracted education: politics in the United States itself.

CHAPTER FOUR

AMERICAN ADMINISTRATOR

As Food Administrator in the direct service of the Government at Washington, and then as Secretary of Commerce in the Cabinet of President Harding and of President Coolidge, Hoover has presented to the American public eye a picture highly confusing. His amazing multiplicity of interests and of endeavors has thoroughly obscured whatever unity of philosophy might lie behind them.

We learn from a public letter written by an ambitious and gratified flour firm that Hoover's energetic young men in the Commerce Department's Bureau of Foreign and Domestic Commerce have contrived in the course of four months to put the firm into happy contact with 2,500 foreign buyers of American flour and have thus managed to enable the firm to accumulate numerous new flour contracts in foreign parts to the total value of more than $2,000,000.

We learn from the newspapers that Hoover desires us to send presents in the form of radio receiving-sets to the lighthouses on our coasts in order that the solitude of our lighthouse-keepers may be solaced by the distant saxophone and beguiled by political speeches on the distress of the farmers.

We learn that under Hoover's inspiration the breath of life has been breathed into a new comprehensive Municipal Code of Building Regulations—a standard code—a model code—suitable for instant adoption by all American cities desiring the very last word of wisdom in economical (but at the same time safe) construction.

We learn that Congress has enacted a law under which Hoover will be permitted and directed to go forth and discover and operate mines or wells of helium gas and then store and hold the gas for use in lighter-than-air airships.

We learn that Hoover has gone to the Southwest to preside over a meeting of the envoys extraordinary and ministers plenipotentiary of the sovereign states of Colorado, Wyoming, Utah, New Mexico, Nevada, Arizona and California for the purpose of arriving at an interstate treaty to impound and to partition the inter-state wasted waters of the Colorado River.

We learn that Hoover is planning a strike by American buyers against foreign price-fixing combinations in rubber, coffee, camphor, sisal, potash, quinine, iodine, nitrates.

We learn that Hoover has changed the locations for traps for salmon at the mouths of the rivers of Alaska.

We learn that Hoover is raising a fund of $20,000,000 to endow learned recluses to look into test-tubes in laboratories and to gaze at star-dust from the tops of mountains in Africa.

We learn that Hoover has sent explorers into Latin America to discover where rubber may be grown in competition with the British rubber from Singapore and the Dutch rubber from Palembang.

We learn that Hoover has issued a report contrasting the merits of a ship-canal to the Atlantic Ocean down the St. Lawrence River with the merits of a ship-canal to the Atlantic Ocean across New York State.

We learn that Hoover is persuading American construction contractors to work in winter as well as in summer on new buildings and on new roads.

We learn that Hoover has developed an organized plan for studying the problem of preserving the grandeur and beauty of Niagara.

We learn that Hoover has presented to Congress, and has secured from Congress, a new law shortening and cheapening the route from the making of inventions to the getting of patents.

We learn that Hoover in the World War Debt

Funding Commission has earnestly and successfully maintained that European Governments
are fully able to repay a large proportion of
their debts to the United States Treasury.

We learn that Hoover has convened a massive
national assemblage of shattered nerves and
harassed brains to try once more to make motor-
cars safer for pedestrians.

We learn that Hoover has turned his oceanic
Bureau of Lighthouses to the task of shedding
illumination upon continental rights-of-way for
aviators.

We learn that Hoover has aroused the manufacturers of hot-water storage-tanks to a get-
together reduction of their types of tanks from
120 to 24.

We learn that Hoover has held a national convention of industrial authorities and of governmental authorities for combating unemployment
by the instant initiation of needed public works.

We learn that Hoover has installed a system
of Stop-and-Go signs for radio-broadcasting-
stations and has become the traffic-cop of the
ether.

We learn that Hoover has objected strenuously and successfully to loans from American
bankers to European monopolies bent upon
extortionate exploitation of American markets.

We learn that Congress has accepted Hoover's recommendations on how to prevent navigable waters from getting polluted by oil.

We learn these things—and many other things—about Hoover; and we are impressed by the Washingtonian witticism to the effect that "Hoover is Secretary of Commerce and Assistant Secretary of Everything Else."

We are also led to inquire:

Is this man simply the world's greatest busybody and meddler, or is he really going somewhere?

In order to answer that question competently, we may go back to observe that a very nice thing to have, if you are seeking a point of destination, is first a point of departure. If you are going to try to get to somewhere, it is well to be sure that you are starting from somewhere.

Hoover, it must be said, does most decidedly start from somewhere. His raids into the unknown are profuse and adventurous but the base from which he flings them out is extraordinarily firm and fixed—and extraordinarily simple and tame.

As soon as he became Secretary of Commerce, he began a study of the commercial problems confronting prospective buyers of homes. Presently—out of that study—a pamphlet was issued entitled "How to Own Your Own

Home.'' The Government Printing Office has sold more than 300,000 copies of it.

Now! What in the world has a Secretary of Commerce to do with homes?

Well! A Secretary of Commerce has to do with business; and business has to do with the construction industry; and the construction industry has to do with the erecting of buildings; and some buildings are homes.

Hoover chose to begin with homes.

It could not be otherwise. His invidualism in business, in government, in religion, I have already pointed out. In his view, a man should have his own economic opportunity; he should have his own local self-rule; he should have his own soul. Naturally, then, he should have the nourishing nest of all of these virtues. He should have his own home.

It is almost sad to have to relate the simplicity and the antiquity of the social thought of this great ''New Economic Prophet of a New Economic Era.''

He prophesies, in truth, no social revolution whatsoever. He prophesies not even any ''reconstruction''—as it is called—of the bases of society. Give him a home, a church, a school. For him they are the eternal and irreplaceable tripod of civil liberty, of government, of national success.

His "progressivism" is only, after all, an utter open-mindedness toward all devices for making that tripod stand steadier and rise higher. His "liberalism" is only a profound conviction that each leg of the tripod must be grounded on freedom. His originality is only an immense and almost miraculous ingenuity in finding for each leg of the tripod an unending supply of new loyalties and new buttresses.

His whole social philosophy can be comprehended and compacted into saying that it goes toward the preservation and perpetuation of the individual home and of the individual personalities within it.

He accordingly forfeits—in my judgment—all claim to be numbered among those statesmen who currently have been able to capture a considerable part of the control of the so-called "progressive wings" of our political parties. They are primarily and prevailingly engaged in contriving vast governmental awnings under which the citizen can be sheltered not only from the sun but from the air. They incessantly proffer to the citizen vast folding beds of ease operated—now down—but at any time up—by the same institution, the same governmental mechanism, which jails people and hangs them. In a word, they make a pilgrimage to the pyramids and return with the Omnipotent State—and call it "progress."

Having done this to that word, they might well be sentenced to keep it. A distinction might now be initiated and maintained between the word "progressive" and the word "liberal." That distinction is pertinent to this narrative and analysis. Hoover views "progressivism" in the light of "liberalism." When "progress" means a new road to restored or confirmed or enlarged liberty, Hoover follows it. When it means a new obstacle to liberty, he avoids it. He goes around it. He moves, but it is not for the mere sake of motion. It is not at all for the sake of novelty. He moves—he moves unrestingly—to retain or to recover the toilsome trail toward what Walt Whitman, American of Americans, had in mind when he said:

"To democracy, the leveler, the unyielding principle of the average, is surely joined another principle. This second principle is individuality, the pride and centripetal isolation of a human being in himself, identity, personalism. It forms, in a sort, or is to form, the compensating balance-wheel of the successful working machine of aggregate America."

Coercivism—the Omnipotent State—is as old as life. Personalism—now called "liberalism"

—is also as old as life. Every statesman stands in the middle of the teeter-totter between those two principles and inclines toward one or the other. Hoover inclines toward "liberalism."

He inclines toward it, however, with both feet. He is not like our contemporary "reactionaries" who want "liberalism" and freedom for their property but "coercivism" and suppression for the speeches of their critics and for the assemblages of their adversaries. So far as Hoover is concerned, if property wants freedom in this country, it will take freedom straight. It will take freedom of speech, freedom of assemblage, freedom of private voluntary organization against the aggressions of wealth right along with the freedom to get wealthy.

Moreover, Hoover inclines toward "liberalism" without forgetting that government itself, though the natural agent of "coercivism," can be made also the conquered agent of an expanding freedom. It is at this point, indeed, that whatever is peculiar, whatever is distinctive, whatever is unique, in his statesmanship begins clearly and emphatically to appear.

Hoover is not content that the state should be negative. He sees for it an abiding and increasing mission that is most deliberately positive. He separates himself there both from our

reactionaries and from those sublime philo-
sophical anarchists who accompany Ralph
Waldo Emerson on the beautiful but wild flight
in which he said:

"The State exists to educate the wise man.
With the appearance of the wise man the State
expires. The appearance of character makes
the State unnecessary."

That flight starts on the ground but ends in
the unsupported void. Hoover, an extreme
"liberal," but also extremely a man of practice,
would say:

"The State exists, yes, to educate the wise
man. That education, however, is endless.
New problems and new situations will necessi-
tate endlessly new classes and courses in it.
Forever and forever the loftiest function of the
State will be to cultivate character and to help it
to unfold itself in its own stimulated nature."

Two applications of this principle by Hoover
may here be noted. As Secretary of Commerce,
he was obliged to deal with the beginnings of
radio broadcasting and with the beginnings of
commercial aviation.

He could have let the radio broadcasting stations acquire a prescriptive private possession
of the ether. He did not do so. He said:

"It would be unfortunate indeed if such an
important function in the distribution of infor-

mation should come under the arbitrary power
of any one group of private persons."

He could—on the other hand—have grasped
the ether arbitrarily for the Government. He
did not do so. He said:

"It would be equally unfortunate if the distribution of information should ever fall into
the hands of the Government."

He could foresee what has happened in
Britain in consequence of the governmentalization there established of broadcasting programs. What has happened is the general
enforced exclusion from those programs in
Britain of the controversial and educative public questions which are here abundantly carried
to our radio audiences.

Hoover avoided both governmentalization
and private monopoly. He avoided governmentalization by issuing licenses freely to
private broadcasting stations. He avoided
private monopoly by issuing those licenses to
numerous and varied interests and—above all
—by restricting every license to a period of
ninety days.

His licenses permitted each interest licensed
to spread its own views with a freedom for
which no government would dare to assume responsibility. Purely private broadcasters
could broadcast Ku Klux Klan programs or

Catholic programs—and did. On the other hand, the shortness of the licenses enabled the Government to retain in its hands the power which Government must always retain over all forms of traffic, whether of motor-cars along the earth or of radio messages through the ether: namely, the power to renew or to terminate a license as "public convenience, interest or necessity" may require.

What, then, has been the outcome? Hoover expressed part of it truly when he said:

"Through the policies which we have established, the Government—and, through the Government, the people—have to-day the control of the channels through the ether, just as they to-day have control of the channels of water-navigation in harbors and rivers."

The other part of the outcome, however, is equally important. Through the policies which have been established in this country the radio broadcasting programs of the United States are left to the adventurousness and to the initiative of the private life of the United States; and thereupon, through the process of trial and error and failure and success with the listeners, our radio broadcasting industry has gone forward to find its own temperament, its own philosophy, its own character.

A similar course has been pursued by Hoover

in the matter of commercial aviation. European Governments have stimulated commercial aviation by subsidies. Hoover declared flatly on this point:

"I do not favor subsidies."

He did, of course, favor paying commercial aviation companies for actual services to the Government—such as the carrying of the mails. The European system, however, of paying commercial aviation companies for carrying private passengers was abhorrent to him. He negatived it here.

His aviation policy nevertheless was no negation merely. He established an Air Information Division in the Department of Commerce. He established an Air Regulations Division. He established an Aeronautical Research Division in the Bureau of Standards. He established an Aeronautical Mapping Section in the Coast and Geodetic Survey. He established the duty of airway-illumination in the Bureau of Lighthouses. In other words, he said to commercial aviation:

"We will educate you through telling you all that we can find out about airplane construction and about aviation practice. We will light you and otherwise protect you from traffic-accidents on your roads through the air. We leave to you the risk of investment and the risk of operation and the risk of choosing the right or wrong cities for your services. Now proceed! Now proceed to show what American pioneering was, and is, and—under this sort of system—always must and will be."

It is, of course, most certainly open to all comers to embrace and to advocate an opposite philosophy. All that is here meant is that the pioneering stock from which Hoover comes has left in Hoover an ineradicable pioneering philosophy.

He follows, however, not simply a part of that philosophy but the whole of it. It is not true that our western pioneers owed to the Government nothing. They owed to it their land. They owed to it their opportunity. They owed to it the scene of their initiative and the furnace of their character.

Similarly, to-day, while Hoover would oblige our modern pioneers to hew out their own clearings in their own new wildernesses, he still would have the Government labor always to spread before private character the opportunity within which—thereupon—and only thereupon —it can fulfill for the United States, by its own exertions, his hard saying:

"National character is but the sum of the moral fiber of individuals."

Hence that strange insistence of his that a

Secretary of Commerce might and should do something about homes.

Having started the launching of the pamphlet on "How to Own Your Own Home," Hoover started many other launchings and sailings in that same direction.

In the course of doing so, he instantly illustrated the distinctive method which he has steadily pursued in all his administrative endeavors. It is a method which flows directly from his repugnance to the merely coercive aspects of government and from his preference for its educative and persuasive possibilities. It is a method therefore which links every public performance with a private voluntary assistance and coöperation.

I have pointed out that in the relief of Belgium and of occupied France Hoover was not content to convey food by alien hands to the hungry. He caused some 50,000 Belgian and French neighbors of the hungry to labor with him coöperatively every day in the accomplishment of his public-private task.

I have pointed out that similarly in Russia he was not content to combat Russian famine with American resources and American directors. He enlisted also the services of 125,000 assisting Russians.

In every country of Central Europe he was constantly pressing upon his subordinates in the American Relief Administration the following proposition:

"An indefinite continuation of our present wide-spread feeding measures would undermine the economic structure and the initiative and the very life of the countries concerned. Therefore every step in the work of the American Relief Administration should be dominated by the determination to create local institutions which will enable each state at the proper moment to undertake its own food policies and arrangements."

The self-help principle that Hoover had attempted to apply in Europe he proceeded to apply with naturally even more conviction in the United States.

Nothing could be falser than the myth which exhibits him as a celestial mental machine on top of a pedestal causing tidal-waves of efficiency to encircle the globe by means of radiations of pure intellect from his solitary head.

He is not such a genius, and he is not such a fool.

I heard him burst into conversation once just after his final return from his efforts in the Mississippi Flood region. What he said was:

"This is about Main Street. What was this

Mississippi Flood?   It was water trying to wash Main Street down and out.

"I suppose I could have called in the whole of the Army.   But what was the use?   All I had to do was to call in Main Street itself.

"I made ninety-one local committees in ninety-one local communities to look after that flood.   That's what I principally did.   And now see!

"I don't think it could have happened in any other country.

"You go to ninety-one different corners—so to speak—of the Main Street of the United States.   You pick up the leading characters just as you find them on each corner.   You say:

" 'A couple of thousand refugees are coming. They've got to have accommodations.   Huts. Water-mains.   Sewers.   Streets.   Dining-halls. Meals.   Doctors.   Everything.   And you haven't got months to do it in.   You haven't got weeks.   You've got hours.   That's my train.'

"So you go away and they go ahead and just simply do it.

"Of all those ninety-one committees there was just one that fell down.

"They say Main Street has no distinction. What is distinction?   Has it anything to do with humanity and with elevation of motive and with capacity for action?

"What is leadership? I call those countries unhappy and unfortunate that are proud of the leadership of a few men. Never will they be able to contend against a country in which almost any man on almost any corner is a potential leader.

"No other Main Street in the world could have done what the American Main Street did in the Mississippi Flood; and Europe may jeer as it pleases at our mass production and our mass organization and our mass education. The safety of the United States is its multitudinous mass leadership."

If Hoover could be brought to examine and to express his inmost ambition, it would be—I think—the precise reverse of the one which has animated and inspired so many of the supermen of history. It would be that when he got through there would be more leaders in his country than when he began.

He was not content, therefore, in the matter of homes, when he had done what the Department of Commerce could do. He was not content when he had established in the Department of Commerce a new Division of Building and Housing. He felt obliged to go on to appoint committees.

If Hoover was told by President Coolidge to go and find a new alternative route for the

Panama Canal, he would not first call for a map or for a tailor to get him a suit of jungle-clothes. He would first telephone the Cosmos Club for any geographical scientists who happened to be there at lunch, and he would appoint a committee.

Hoover can mar the romance of any undertaking by filling it so full of committees that nobody can ever find out any striking individual thing that anybody ever did in it.

He is all for individualism; but it seems to mean that every individual has a right to be on a committee. Some people's individualism means "the survival of the fittest." Hoover's means the utilization of all the fit.

He now has more than 4,500 local committees in this country giving demonstrations and instructions for the building of "Better Homes."

This he does through the purely private and voluntary organization called "Better Homes in America," of which he is President.

These local committees build model homes and show them. They do not work for the seller. They work for the buyer. They work particularly for the young husband and wife just starting out. In 1923 a half of the houses which they built and showed cost some $7,000 apiece. Last year their average model house cost less than $4,500.

Tirelessly these committees have preached and have stimulated residential construction. They have not been without their influence—it is sure—in the renewed popularity of residential construction in this country. In 1920 only 27 per cent. of our total American construction of edifices was residential. In the last year of record that percentage had risen to 48; and the value of the new contracts for homes was in that year almost two and a half billions of dollars.

Hoover could justify his interest in the matter by calling attention to the admirable commercial results. He also could—and did—justify it more seriously by remarking:

"In the United States, as in most other modern nations, many groups of people have food and clothing and many luxuries and yet they have not good shelter. The character of a people is largely affected by the homes in which they dwell. In the restless currents of our modern life we are sometimes at a loss for ideals to help us keep our bearings. A higher and finer type of home is one ideal to which we can well hold fast."

An "ideal"!

Hence Hoover's idealistic appointment of his dreary Advisory Committee on Building Codes. Hence the idealistic and dismally detailed recommendations whereby that Committee proceeded to cheapen the construction of safe brick walls by—I think—13 per cent. A satirist could easily see Hoover calculating out—somehow— the number of children in the United States whose parents, because of new economical practices permitted under revised municipal building codes, have been able to build nurseries for them.

When homes get built, however, there is a tendency among commercial and industrial buildings to move out among them and ruin them for family life. Hence Hoover's appointment of his Advisory Committee on Zoning. Hence the publication—by the business men and lawyers and city-planners on this Committee— of their "Zoning Primer." Hence the release of this "Primer" in installments to the reading public through the National Association of Real Estate Boards. Hence the development of a "Standard State Zoning Enabling Act" which has been used in the formulation of the zoning legislation of some thirty states. Hence a heap of technical considerations and conclusions from which the winds of the news can blow off only a swirl of blinding details as dry as dust.

It is profoundly characteristic. Hoover is always doing some grubby chore in furtherance of some sentimental idea (like homes for chil-

dren to live in and zoned districts for them to
play in) ; and the sentimentality in question is
almost invariably just as commonplace as the
chore is grubby.

Hoover does not at all see the citizen as needing first a university course in the higher civics.
He sees him as needing first a home, a job, and
a chance to get ahead, himself.

Here lies the deep difference between Hoover
and the run of "reformers."

Your regular "reformer" sees principally
some evil-doer and rises betimes in the morning
to slay him with the teeth of a muck-rake.

Hoover seldom starts with the iniquity of
the evil-doer. He almost always starts with the
opportunity that should be afforded to the ordinary normal man. He seems to entertain the
comforting conviction that normality, if given
a chance, will swamp iniquity. The primary
direction of his statesmanship has been simply
toward creating new channels of opportunity
for normality.

He is not dominantly a "reformer." He is
more a "former."

This is especially clear in the endeavor which
has most especially claimed his attention as Secretary of Commerce: namely, the prevention of
"waste" in American economic life.

Hoover has listed thirteen sorts of waste which he alleges to be prevalent among us to our great discredit as a "business nation." He has stated further that:

"I am disposed to agree with a recent report of the Engineering Council that these wastes amount in many lines to 25 or 30 per cent. of the cost paid by the consumer or producer."

He always, however, at once adds:

"In speaking of waste I do not mean waste in the sense of willful waste. I do not mean the waste that any single individual can correct. I mean the waste that can only find remedy in collective action. Our industrial and distribution services are individually of high efficiency. It is in their collective action that we can seek progress."

Ominous word, "collective"! It might seem to portend a new law. It might seem to portend it particularly because, in Hoover's list of wastes, there appears the following:

"Waste due to unfair practices of a small minority."

Shall we not then pass a new law against that small minority? Ultimately, perhaps, Hoover would say; but, first, something else.

Let us take a quick look at that something else in one basic industry: lumber.

It is a story which may stand as the epitome

of the whole of Hoover's anti-waste program and performance—an epitome of dark and intricate economic detail brought to a clear moral and political outcome.

Two of the wastes listed by Hoover have been extremely conspicuous in the lumber industry.

One is: "Waste from deficient standards of quality and grades."

The other is: "Waste from unnecessary multiplication of trade terms, sizes and varieties."

In the lumber industry there have been at least ten or a dozen different thicknesses for the one-inch board. How thick was a one-inch board when you ordered it? One inch. How thick was it when you got it? Almost any thickness except one inch.

For such reasons there was always an earnest push in Congress for what might be called a "pure lumber" law—a law which should prescribe the dimensions of pieces of lumber, just as federal law now already does in fact prescribe that a standard apple-barrel shall be seventeen and one-eighth inches across the diameter of its head and sixty-four inches on the circumference of its bulge.

Hoover said:

"Unless the lumber industry does something for itself, it will get something like that done

to it—something embedded in the rock of the
law beyond all ready reach of the flexibility of
life.''

In 1922 the lumber industry thereupon asked
him to summon a conference. It can be said
that he inspired the conference. He did. It
can be said that he put the Government in the
position of being the host to the conference. He
did. He desired, he accepted, for the Government, in this matter, the task of moral leadership. He thereupon expected the industry to
comb its own hair and wash its own face. It
did.

A first conference was held, and then a second, and then a third. To the third came virtually every element in any way responsibly concerned.

Consumers were represented by delegates
from such institutions as the Association of
Wood-using Industries and the National Association of Purchasing Agents.

The technique of construction was represented by delegates from such institutions as
the American Institute of Architects, the Associated General Contractors and the American
Society of Civil Engineers.

Retailers and wholesalers of lumber were
represented by delegates from their national
societies and from their state societies.

The lumber-producers themselves were represented by delegates from the National Lumber Manufacturers' Association and by delegates from the specialized associations speaking for the hemlock of the North, the cypress of the South, the redwood of California, the pine of North Carolina, and so on.

It was really a Lumber Legislature, a Lumber Constitutional Convention, unspectacularly called a conference.

By this conference the number of different sizes and sorts of lumber to be carried in lumber-yards was reduced nearly 60 per cent. That was millions and millions of dollars a month of savings. Further—and much more importantly—definitions were found and declared for defects in lumber and for grades of lumber. That was the founding of recognized collective custom, of admitted and expected standards, of ethics, in lumber.

Thereafter, for instance, if a lumber producer said that his product contained "small knots," he would be held definitely to mean that the knots were more than one-half inch but not more than three-quarters of an inch in diameter. Thereafter, also, for instance, if he said "one-inch board," he would be held to mean definitely —something.

But what? That was the great legislative

issue in the Third General Lumber Conference
of the United States.

It seemed to be agreed on all hands that the
one-inch board had sunk so far from being one-
inch that there was no hope ever of restoring it
to parity. It had to be "stabilized"—so to
speak—like a depreciated currency—at a lower
level.

A strong faction emerged in favor of $^{25}\!/_{32}$
of an inch as the new standard. The Forest
Products Laboratory of the United States, on
the other hand, had committed itself to $^{26}\!/_{32}$.
The two factions conducted a spirited and eloquent debate on the issue between them—which
was $\frac{1}{32}$ of an inch.

It was very hard on the newspaper corre-
spondents. Still, it might have been worse.
The political point of the whole matter was:

If that debate had not been held among lum-
berites who knew something about it, it would
have had to be held some day among Congressmen knowing nothing about it.

Somebody had to legislate for the industry:
either Congress or the industry itself. The industry itself was now doing it.

The $^{25}\!/_{32}$ faction and the $^{26}\!/_{32}$ faction could
not agree. Thereupon a sub-committee of five
manufacturers and five retailers held a night
session. The next day both factions won, when

agreement was had to the effect that $^{25}\!/_{32}$ should be the thickness of the standard one-inch lumber-yard board and that $^{26}\!/_{32}$ should be the thickness of the standard one-inch industrial board.

That agreement became Article Twenty-four in the new Bible of Lumber Ethics.

The forbidding full title of that Bible is:

"United States Department of Commerce; Revised Simplified Practice Recommendation Number Sixteen; Lumber; Issued by the Bureau of Standards; Accepted by the Associations, Societies and Groups Listed Herein."

Modern governments have always issued big books containing supposed wisdom for the guidance of their subjects or citizens. Hoover's ingenious and penetrating novelty is to get the subjects or citizens to agree upon the wisdom which they then pledge their honor collectively and individually to obey. The ultimately distinctive and operating part of a Hoover report on Simplified Practice is the words:

"Accepted by the Associations, Societies and Groups Listed Herein."

The lumber report was accepted overwhelmingly by the principal associations of producers, wholesalers, retailers, architects, contractors, and industrial users.

The commandments laid down in it came to a

total number of one hundred and fifty-four. Twenty-four of them were more than commandments. They went toward the actual effective enforcement of commandments. They established—and then applied—the following principle:

"The responsibility of the entire organized lumber industry for the maintenance of agreed and published sizes and grades and inspection standards is recognized."

To that end each association within the lumber industry was committed to the establishment and to the maintenance of an inspection service within its own field, and the whole industry was committed to the continued maintenance of a Central Committee on Lumber Standards at Washington.

With what results? They may be compressed into one statement:

There is a general compliance with the one hundred and fifty-four self-imposed commandments of "Revised Simplified Practice Recommendation Number Sixteen," and there is in Congress no further agitation worth mentioning for any law to regulate the dimensional ethics or the measurement morals of lumbermen.

Roosevelt gave us a law on pure food. It was much needed. Hoover has gone far toward

giving us pure lumber without a law. It is a
step toward the era which he is always persuading himself he sees coming: "the era of self-
governing industry."

"Political legislative action," he has said,
"is always clumsy."

"I am one of those," he has said, "who believe in the sub-stratum of inherent honesty in
our citizenship."

The principles and methods thereupon which
he set going in lumber he has set going also in
some eighty other commodities. The stagger-
ing and stupefying statistics involved are of
secondary importance in a narrative leading
toward political and social conclusions. Let it
be that the number of items in builders' hard-
ware has been reduced from 6,948 to 5,130. Let
it be that the number of types of grinding
wheels has been reduced from 715,200 to 254,-
400. Let it be that the savings effected amount
to whatever number of hundreds of millions of
dollars a year it is. I take it that the one statis-
tic that has lasting public significance in this
whole phase of Hoover's activities is the following:

His publicly owned and operated Division of
Simplified Practice, with a staff of only some
twenty persons, is the channel for the free collective deliberations and decisions of more than

five hundred groups of American private business men. Seldom has there been so little government used to let loose so much free will.

Using government to help these groups to
govern themselves, Hoover also, however, uses
these groups to help government.

In his publicly owned and operated Bureau of
Standards, dealing with scientific experiments
and inventions, he now has some eighty "advisory committees" from private industrial
associations. He also has, from such associations, some sixty-two representatives working
as research-scholars in the Bureau of Standards laboratories. All the scientific results
thus secured, all the scientific advances thus
made, become the common property of all
American industry and of the whole American
nation. Public routine gets enlivened with private initiative. Private initiative gets lifted to
the general good.

It becomes perfectly clear accordingly that
Hoover as an administrator is not concluded
and dismissed when he is called an administrator. He has not been simply administrative.
He has not merely turned wheels. He has called
into being new social forces for the turning of
the wheels. He has been—in the deepest sense
—political. He has established among us a
fundamental and audacious political novelty.

He has evolved the private-public Governmental Department. He has evoked the public-private business citizen.

He could not very well escape this outcome. He had been destined to it by his dread of unrestrained government. He had been destined to it by his method of always working through associates, by his passion for committees, by his delight in depending upon organization.

He was inexorably destined—in the end—to be a full-flowered "organization man" in politics itself.

As a political correspondent, I have a natural prejudice against political amateurs. It is bad enough to have to report the prima-donnas of public life without having to report those of them who are either so incompetent or so conceited that they cannot or will not sing on key.

Politics is a thing that requires some unison. If I wished to be unkind, I could mention many noble and futile characters who are now in private life because they thought politics was a game of solitaire.

It is all a dream to think that George Washington put Alexander Hamilton and Thomas Jefferson into his Cabinet as Secretary of the Treasury and as Secretary of State simply because of his esteem for their ability. Robert

Morris was more experienced in finance than Hamilton. John Adams was more experienced in foreign affairs than Jefferson. Washington put Hamilton and Jefferson into his Cabinet because they were the operating heads of our two great original political factions. He put them into it because he wanted both factions right where he could see them all the time. In other words, his motive was thoroughly political.

Washington gave to this country an almost errorless administration. He could withstand at need the intrigues of cliques and the frenzies of mobs. He had grounded himself on a balanced and comprehensive estimate not only of the country's problems but also of its social elements and sentiments. He had fortified himself not only with righteousness but also with associations among those who—so unrighteously—did not entirely agree with him. The public man who does not do so and who imagines that he can resist cliques and mobs with his own sole virtue and valor may be greater than Washington but his retirement from office will not be like Washington's—voluntary—and his greatness will be for exhibition only to his mirror.

Hoover has admirers who glory in asserting that he is a great public man but "no politician." This is like asserting that he is a great engineer but "no mathematician." It is like asserting that a man is a wonderful designer of bridges, only he cannot calculate the strains and stresses which his bridges must meet. It is like asserting that a man is a great general, only he cannot get any troops that are for him.

Public men who are not politicians remain in public life at the mere sufferance of public men who are. The administrator who only manicures the public coral-reef is kept on it—and can at any time be hurled off from it into the deep sea—by the recognizer and organizer of our free and willful human coral-insects.

There is only one real freedom in politics. It is that of the actual—and successful—politician. It is that of the man who through some deference to others has found followers and who thereupon through some submergence of self has found leadership. In the politics of a democracy it never can—and, for that matter, never should—cease to be true that public success for an individual citizen depends upon a reasonable deflation of the ego and a reasonable recollection of the divine paradox that "whosoever shall seek to save his life shall lose it, and whosoever shall lose his life shall preserve it."

In politics, however, it is absolutely necessary to discriminate between two things often identified but always separable. One thing is political manners. The other thing is political methods.

William McKinley was a perfected practitioner of political manners and political methods both. He could with equal address make a friend by a costless turn of a word or carry a state by a harmless twist of a measure.

It was his methods, however, that were essential and not his manners. I have observed many men who had wonderful political manners but who, while they were charming a few people by their words and looks, were alienating a multitude by their acts. Indeed, the "good fellow" in politics—like Warren Gamaliel Harding—is often betrayed to his own hurt because his attention to political manners and to the pleasing of his acquaintances has diverted him unduly from the doing of those acts—sometimes ruthless— which would conciliate the good will of that infinitely larger number of people whom he personally could never know or meet.

I would say flatly that the politician who thinks more about the few people he meets than about the many people he does not meet is simply no politician at all.

In consonance with this view it can be observed that it most certainly does happen that many successful politicians are positively deficient in personal political manners.

Few of them, of course, have ever been quite so extreme in this matter as Benjamin Harrison who contrived to become President in spite of the high degree of truth in the witticism to the effect that he could say "yes" in a tone more irritating than anybody else's "no" and that with a hand-shake intended to be friendly he could make an enemy for life.

Washington's manners, however, were certainly to many people at least distinctly frigid and repelling, and Jackson's to many people were outrightly warmly offensive and infuriating. As for John Quincy Adams, he had the manners of—an Adams. The Adamses—father and son—rose to the Chief Magistracy of the American Republic with manners which for aloofness and remoteness were regarded as beyond presidential precedent and regarded also as beyond all possible presidential repetition until their unexhausted state of Massachusetts —there she stands!—proved in our own days that she could do it all over again without the slightest exertion.

The man nevertheless who can meet Calvin Coolidge and who, upon noting that Mr. Coolidge makes no effort to enchant him, can conclude that here is a Nathanael and here is an Israelite in whom there is no political guile may be making—perhaps—some slight error.

The same error is abundantly made about Hoover.

It is true, of course, that on the point of political manners Hoover is possibly a shade deeper in the shadow than Mr. Coolidge himself.

Mr. Coolidge could at least go to houses in Northampton and knock on the front doors and not retreat till he had said: "I'm running for Councilman." He could also sit all by himself in a room in the Adams Hotel in Boston and be right there, doing nothing, when a citizen-visitor dropped in.

Hoover, when he has talked to a radio audience about the social implications of railroad rates on wheat from Yankton, South Dakota, to Galveston, Texas, has got about as far toward an easy and familiar soliciting of votes as he can ever get; and, as for his hospitality to citizen-visitors in his office, the trouble is precisely that he is never—never—doing nothing.

Moreover, whatever it was that he was doing before you came in, he seems usually to be still more or less thinking about it while you are talking to him.

He additionally makes those marks of which I have spoken—those patterns—on pieces of paper—while you are talking to him.

An admiring young engineer once went to see

him. He carried with him, naturally, a sort of romantic respect for "the most famous engineer in the world." He anticipated—at the same time—and just the same—a sort of cozy fraternal chat with a fellow-engineer. He returned and was interrogated by his friends.

"What did the great man say to you?"

" 'Good morning.' "

"Yes. What else?"

" 'Unh! Unh!' "

"Yes. Yes. What else?"

"Nothing."

"Then why did you stay fifteen minutes?"

"I'll tell you. He had a piece of paper. When I came in, he drew a circle on it. I talked for a while, and stopped, and he drew a radius from the center of the circle to the circumference. I looked at that radius and started again. When I stopped again, he drew another radius. I became absolutely interested. I said to myself: 'That circle is as long as I'm supposed to stay.' So I kept on talking and stopping; and he kept on filling up the circle; and he made seventeen radii; and there was room for just one more; and when he put that one in, I left. I got a lot off my chest and he's got a picture of a cart-wheel with eighteen spokes in it. That's all."

It would seem to be enough; and any observer

who will not distinguish between political manners and political methods may say about such
a man, precisely as he most certainly would
have said about Calvin Coolidge in Northampton in 1899:

"What for a politician is that?"

Yet Mr. Coolidge was destined to some considerable achievements as a politician; and a
picture of Hoover's manners unaccompanied by
a picture of the results of Hoover's methods is
an utterly deceitful optical illusion.

His methods as an administrator—I have already pointed out—are in themselves of the
very essence of democratic popular politics.
They rest—as I have already indicated—not at
all upon arbitrary personal edicts. They rest
upon conferences and conventions and committees, upon association and coöperation and
organization.

What is a politician's "machine"? It is
nothing in the world but a few people in each
precinct who have been associated with him in
endeavors which he may have initiated or con-
summated but which they have shared.

Hoover, in virtually every county in every
state in the whole United States, now has more
than a few people who have been associated
with him—distantly, perhaps—intimately, perhaps—in some committee or sub-committee or

sub-sub-committee having to do with the promoting of waterways or the feeding of poor
Poles or the improving of statistics or the establishing of clinics for ailing children or the saving of sawdust in lumber-mills or the rescuing
of flood-victims or the preventing of business
"booms" or the stopping of business "slumps"
or the restoring of employment or the propagat-
ing of game-fish or the simplifying of ware-
house-receipts or the appointing of bright
young men to scholarships in Europe or for
something else humanitarian or profitable or
both.

Some of the people thus drawn into contact
with Hoover's activities have disliked them and
have become his enemies. Others have liked
them so much that they have become his almost
slavish and ludicrous adulators. It is a safe
calculation that the mass of them have been
moved neither to enmity nor to adulation but
simply to a much less vivid but much more important state of mind: namely, a sheer habitude
of regarding him as a leader.

It is that habitude—and not his "efficiency"
—that is his chief asset as an American public
man.

The Department of Commerce is one of the
smallest of federal governmental departments.
The head of it could be "efficient" with every

"efficiency" ever devised and charted by the able editor of *System Magazine* and yet never make a dent upon the consciousness of the electorate of the United States.

It is really a weariness of the mind to listen to the talk about Hoover's "efficiency." Lincoln's Secretary of War, Stanton, was so "efficient" that the eye ached to behold him; and that was where he stopped. Nobody ever even accused Lincoln of "efficiency"; and he will never stop. The American people do not choose —and the excellent and splendid chances are that they will never choose—their supreme leaders for "efficiency."

Senator Penrose of Pennsylvania on this topic once brought a bewildered confusion to a delegation of business men in Washington from his state. They wanted "a business man for President." Penrose was widely misunderstood. He was widely—in fact—maligned. He was no more afraid of his campaign contributors than of any other human beings. He said to the delegation:

"You want a business man for President. Let's take the best one in the country—the one that's made the most money. Let's take Rockefeller."

"Heavens, no," said the delegation.

"Then let's take the next most successful," said Penrose. "Ford."

"God," said the delegation with prompt and regrettable but irrepressible profanity and horror.

"Then go home," said Penrose abruptly, and dismissed them.

Penrose was aiming at a great truth. That truth was that "efficiency" in and of itself does not in any way prove that a man is qualified for high office; because it does not in any way prove that he has discerned the soul of a country or can divine its destiny.

It is obvious that the first sure step toward that discernment and toward that divination is to be found in a search for contacts with one's fellow-citizens quite outside of the compulsions which exist between employer and employee or which exist between Department head and Department clerk.

It is equally obvious that Hoover through his coöperative committee-system has sought those contacts and has acquired them to an extent unprecedented and unparalleled in American federal governmental history.

Those contacts thereupon have three absolutely inevitable political consequences.

In the first place, they keep Hoover instantly and continuously aware of the country's movements and moods. They compensate him for one of the gaps in his equipment. They compensate him for not being politically the most intuitive man in Washington. They bring it about that without any question he is politically the best informed.

In the second place, they give him in most sections of the country a multitude of local followers who exhort their fellow-citizens to go to the polls and vote for him and who thus in various primary elections have produced on his behalf what is fancifully called a "popular uprising" but what realistically is the direct political result of previous public-service "organization."

In the third place, they produce for him—when he needs it—a powerful popular pressure upon Congress for such legislation as he may reluctantly discover to be desirable and may thereupon formally recommend.

He has carried some twenty-four legislative proposals to the attention of Congress. He has secured the enactment of some twenty of them into laws.

Few administrators in Washington have ever been so steadily victorious on Capitol Hill. The inhabitants of the Hill are all of them politicians. Is Hoover's success among them nonpolitical?

In view of the grotesque and ignoble travesty which passes in some people's minds for the whole of politics, it would be pleasant to say "yes."

In view of what politics in its larger bearings actually is, it is necessary to say "no."

The larger bearings of politics have relatively little to do with hand-shakes. They have relatively much to do with services and with loyalties.

A Massachusetts manufacturer once formed a very unfavorable opinion of Calvin Coolidge. Mr. Coolidge was then in the Massachusetts legislature. The manufacturer went to Boston to see him. He asked him to do some legislative chore or other on behalf of—I think—some educational institution.

Mr. Coolidge evinced no interest. He volunteered no assistance. The manufacturer went away extremely disgusted.

He made, however, one mistake. He failed to keep track of what the legislature was doing. So, after hearing nothing from Mr. Coolidge for several weeks, he again went to Boston and again asked Mr. Coolidge to do the chore. Mr. Coolidge's reply crushed him to earth. It was:

"I did that right after you were here last time."

Examination of the record proved this to be precisely true. The manufacturer proceeded thereupon to make his successful way toward being a Coolidge delegate in the next Republican National Convention. His state of mind was natural. He had got a service. He had got it without being soft-soaped in advance. He had got it without being asked for gratitude afterwards. He had just simply got it—impersonally—as a sheer bare fact. He was fascinated. He was captured for keeps.

Hoover, as a Department head, has exhibited a quite similar tendency toward silent but delivered services.

Hoover's Department—like every other Department—serves the public not only directly but also through Congress. Most ordinary citizens who think they need anything from the Government write to their Congressmen. The Congressmen write, or go, to the appropriate Department.

The Department can begin unrolling red tape into an endless belt conveyor that will keep a Congressman going round and round for years. It can also give him a frozen shoulder and a lofty stare which means: "You politician, how dare you come around here among us public servants?"

Bureaucrats are always seeing iniquity in politicians. Politicians are always seeing insolence in bureaucrats.

This is one of the reasons why few Department heads ever become formidable candidates for the presidency. They live in Washington; and in Washington, on the whole, the political set and the bureaucratic set live in a state of chronic mutual jealousy and hostility.

Hoover might have been expected to express that hostility with an especial fervor. He was such a political novice! He was such a scientific engineer!

Indubitably in Washington his first feelings toward politicians were as if toward animals of another species. Their way of thinking simultaneously about a thing's merits and about a thing's political necessities seemed to him to have small relationship to thought.

Indubitably, also, the first feelings of politicians in Washington toward him were of pained and almost incredulous surprise at his very existence. His way of thinking—at times —like a ray of pure reason through an incandescent tube in a laboratory seemed to them to have small relationship to life.

He had been trained to regard them as a political machine. They most certainly at once regarded him as a mental machine. How could

these two machines ever get geared to each
other?

In the first place, Hoover learned something
that did him a lot of good. He made an amazing discovery. It was amazing to him. He con-
fided it to a friend. The only really amazing
thing about it was its literal—though seldom
appreciated—truth. Hoover said:

"I've been watching those people on the Hill.
I've been talking with them—or listening to
them—a lot. What do you think? Why are
they in politics? I've found out. They don't
make any money. They work hard. They
study the people all the time. They have to
gamble all the time on what the people think
and want. They are always putting up their
careers as the stakes on the returns. They're
sports. They like the game. They love the
thrill. They serve their constituents; and
what's the most that most of them ever get out
of it? What's the most that most of them ever
even want out of it? Just what I've mentioned.
The thrill of the game!"

In other words, Hoover, with his realism,
soon cleared his head of the myth that politics
is a sort of Dante's Inferno. He soon saw
politics as simply part of that general human
world which for him—as I have noted—is not
so much a place for hunting the wicked as for

cherishing and forwarding the interests and aspirations of ordinary people, ordinarily reasonably selfish, ordinarily reasonably decent.

With this discovery about politics made, Hoover's delight in "organization" could come into full action.

Congressmen began to find that action was what they got from his Department.

I asked a Congressman not long ago why he was making speeches for Hoover. I have to report that his first reason was the following experience of his own:

He comes from a seashore district. He has constituents who make their living by fishing. They often encounter fogs. In these fogs they sometimes lose themselves. Some of them have lost themselves forever. The land has seen them no more. The survivors wanted some sort of signaling device out on the water to warn them of rocks and to guide them to the channels. They wanted a whistling-buoy—or the like.

The Congressman went to the Department having such matters in charge—namely, the Department of Commerce. He found that there was no appropriation directly and immediately applicable toward what he wanted. He talked to Hoover. Hoover listened to him as if he just about half heard him. The Congressman cal-

culated that he would have to persuade the
Bureau of the Budget and the Appropriations
Committees of the Senate and of the House and
the Bureau of Lighthouses in the Department
of Commerce and Hoover for several years.

What actually happened was that the buoy
was in place on the water in the Congressman's
district in three weeks.

The Congressman was frank to say that he
had seldom got a word of personal interest out
of Hoover but he was eloquent on Hoover's cut-
tings of red tape to meet the legitimate and
proved needs of his district.

This spring more than a hundred Congressmen declared themselves outrightly for Hoover
for President. The inward politics of that fact
is that it never could have happened if Hoover
had fallen into the bureaucratic error of treat-
ing Congressmen as natural incurable enemies
to departmental efficiency. He has treated
them, on the contrary, as natural legitimate
customers for his Department's proper services.

But if Hoover has been honorably political on
the point of services, he has been equally honorably political on the point of loyalties.

On this latter point he has been increasingly
unsatisfactory to those political observers who
judge a public man not so much by his own

morals as by the time he spends washing those
of other people. Hoover is a poor denouncer.
He does not denounce the White House. He
does not denounce the Cabinet. He does not denounce the Party. He does not denounce
Congress.

Nobody can successfully charge him with doing any improper thing for White House or
Cabinet or Party or Congress. On the other
hand, nobody can successfully make out that he
has ever summoned those institutions to choose
between obeying him and losing him.

The truth is that for weal or woe he is
thoroughly and without equivocation a "party
man." He has with the utmost explicitness
said:

"It is true that progress requires that men
shall advocate their ideas by every means possible. Likewise, however, the compromise necessary for successful government requires that
they should advance those ideas within one
party or the other. I know that political purists
and logicians jibe at such a conception. Nevertheless it is a talent for tempering logic with
compromise that has made our institutions
workable."

His own words in this matter can be supple-
mented by those of a much more politically professional person. If a "party man" ever lived

among us, it was and is John T. Adams of Iowa,
former Chairman of the Republican National
Committee. He began with regarding Hoover
as a specimen of some peculiarly offensive breed
of "mugwump." He ended by saying about
him:

"Hoover is a firm believer in party organization and the American party system of government. He fully understands, out of his experience as one of the successful organizers of this
age, the value of organization. As applied to
party government, he appreciates the necessity
of coöperation between the party organization
and the party administration in order to pro-
mote the policies and principles for which the
party stands."

These observations by Mr. Adams are simply
undeniably accurate. There are public men
whose value to society is in doing good against
a party. There are public men whose value to
society is in doing good through a party. Hoover belongs without question to the latter class.

The merit of the former class is in producing
an occasional wholesome chaos. The merit of
the latter class is in producing steady orderly
results. Hoover has secured from Congress an
array of results which never could have been
acquired except through the services and loyalties which he has rendered and displayed.

Congressmen have cheerfully provided him with generous appropriations for the work of his Department. They customarily—though the public does not seem to know it—are more economical than the Bureau of the Budget in their consideration of the needs of the Departments. They customarily shave down the departmental financial estimates made to them by the Bureau of the Budget. For Hoover's Department of Commerce they have almost always revised those estimates upwards.

In 1921, when he started, they gave him less than one and one-half million dollars for his Department's Bureau of Foreign and Domestic Commerce. This year they gave him for it more than four million dollars.

They also—as I have indicated—are in the habit of passing his laws for him. He has been extremely chary in the promoting of laws but he has been obliged to see a necessity for them on a considerable number of topics such as, for instance, trade in China, customs statistics, cotton statistics, aviation, radio, potash-mines, helium-wells, patents, river pollution, salmon fisheries, halibut fisheries, steamboat inspection, and (above all) the establishment of an American "Foreign Commerce Service" on a reasonably equal plane of dignity with our foreign political diplomatic service.

Legislation on all of those topics has been granted to Hoover on terms exactly or approximately in line with his expressed views.

It is ridiculous in such circumstances to exhibit him as an amateur political guerrilla. He has done what many of our very best professionals in administrative office have failed to do. He has "got along with Congress."

As an administrator, then, we have observed him in his relations to the public and we have observed him in his relations to the politicians. We have noted that in each case, impersonal as he may be in his manners, he tends in his methods toward the amplest use of the personal binding contacts of "organization."

It remains to consider the relations which he has sustained in Washington toward foreign countries. We shall here again note an apparent contradiction. We shall note that Hoover, however international in experience, is in conduct nationalistic almost to a fault.

His relations in Washington toward foreign countries began when he became United States Food Administrator in 1917. It is in the light of foreign demands that his record as Food Administrator must be principally read.

I have spoken of his efforts in Paris on behalf of American producers of hogs who had

been encouraged to production by his Food-
Administration price-promises. The other basic
commodity produced under such promises was
wheat.

No part of Hoover's career has been the subject of more controversy than the wheat chapter
in it. Yet that chapter can be condensed into
two paragraphs.

One. Hoover got for the American wheat-
farmer less money than the American wheat-
farmer wanted to get.

Two. Hoover made our European Allies pay
a great deal more money for American wheat
than our European Allies wanted to pay.

The pertinent facts are extremely few and
extremely clear.

The 1916 wheat crop—almost all of it—
passed from the farmer at less than $1.40 a
bushel.

In 1917, when Hoover became Food Administrator, the middlemen in wheat had caused the
price of wheat to soar among themselves from
high level to higher level of speculation.

The Allies thereupon united all British buying and all French buying and all Italian buying
into one monopolistic centralized buying agency
called the Wheat Export Company. They declared that the price they should pay for wheat
in the United States would be in the neighbor-

hood of $1.50 a bushel.   They declared with truth that the price of wheat in Australia and in India was below that figure.

Hoover thereupon requested the President to appoint a committee to determine a fair price for wheat.   This committee had twelve members.   Six of them—like Mr. Barrett of the Farmers' Union and Mr. Taber of the Grange —were direct representatives of agricultural interests.   Two of them—Mr. Doak of the Railway Trainment and Mr. Sullivan of the Brooklyn Federation of Labor—were direct representatives of labor interests.

Hoover was not a member of the committee. He gave the committee no advice.

The labor men on the committee maintained that the fair price for No. 1 northern spring wheat at Chicago should be $1.84 a bushel.   The committee fixed it at $2.20.   This was seventy cents above what the Allies thought was fair to the Allied armies in the field against the common German foe.   It was thirty-six cents above what the labor men thought was fair to the American consumer.

It was so profitable to the wheat-farmer that the following things took place:

Our amount of land planted to wheat in the average of the five years just preceding the war had been 51 million acres.   In 1917 it rose to 58 million acres. In 1918 it rose to 64 million acres. In 1919 it rose to 76 million acres.

A parallel rise took place in the value of land in our principal wheat area.

In our West North Central States of Kansas, Nebraska, Missouri, Iowa, South Dakota, North Dakota and Minnesota the average price of farm-land per acre in 1914 had been $64. In 1917 it rose to $75. In 1918 it rose to $83. In 1919 it rose to $91.

The wheat-farmer fared better—much better —than his average fellow-citizen.

Take the prices of the period immediately preceding the war as the base for calculation. Call that base 100. By Armistice Day the relative price of wheat was 245. The relative price of all other commodities put together was only 210.

The wheat farmer fared better—much better —than the people who bought his wheat from him and made it into flour.

The wheat-farmer, as we have seen, got a big lift in the price of wheat. The flour manufacturer got a big drop in the price of flour. The price of flour had been $18 a barrel. Hoover squeezed it down to $13 a barrel. That was elevating and expanding the farmer while squeezing and depressing the middleman and the flour-manufacturer.

It was necessary also to squeeze and to depress the treasuries of the Allied Governments.

The citizens of the Allied countries could not afford to pay the price for wheat fixed as fair by President Wilson's committee and enforced by Hoover's Food Administration. The Allied Governments were thereupon obliged to put part of the burden of that price on their treasuries. They bought our wheat at the price we exacted and sold it below cost to their people to keep them alive.

It would seem that if anybody was really entitled on this point to a grudge against the United States Food Administration it was Allied Europe.

It may also be noted that from this time forward the name of Hoover raised less and less of any storm of applause in British and French and Italian governmental circles.

Hoover was to come to the day when the London *Morning Post* would accuse him of advising our farmers after the war to restrict their wheat-acreage and their wheat-production in order to raise prices and enrich America by starving the peoples of Europe.

He was to come to the day when the London *Times*—in the matter of his onslaught on British Malayan rubber prices—would say that he was "making himself ridiculous in the eyes of the world."

He opposed American governmental loans at the end of the war to European industrial and commercial interests when such loans were earnestly advocated as the only conceivable means of saving Europe from destitution, dissolution and death. He prophesied that the death would not come and he successfully advocated—in place of loans to European buyers—loans to American coöperative societies of agricultural producers to enable them to hold their products for fair world-prices.

He set up a new Transportation Division in the Bureau of Foreign and Domestic Commerce of the Commerce Department for the principal purpose of promoting American waterways in order to enable American agriculture to compete more successfully with the agriculture of Australia, of India, of Argentina, in world-markets. He pointed out that the wheat-farmer of Argentina is closer to the seaboard than the wheat-farmer of the United States. He pointed out that accordingly on each ton of wheat the recent world-wide increase in freight rates has moved the Argentine farmer only 117 cents farther away from Liverpool while it has moved the South Dakota farmer 408 cents farther away. He calculated that the improvement of

the Missouri River would more than reëqualize
South Dakota with Argentina on the Liverpool
wheat-docks. His American waterway development plans were direct endeavors toward a
more agressive agricultural Americanism in the
international competitive field.

He at the same time—by a turn which his
European critics were quick to detect and denounce—abated not one jot of his inherited Republican passion for keeping the "home market" thoroughly protected against competi-
tively "destructive" foreign goods. He insist-
ently advocated and defended high—and even
higher—tariff duties. He pointed with pride to
the fact that under a higher tariff duty our
plantings of flax had increased from a million
acres to three million acres and the value of
the crop produced had increased from 22 million
dollars to 68 million dollars. He demanded a
similarly effective protection for our producers
of wool and of milk and cream and cheese and
of vegetable oils and of numerous other agricultural commodities. He maintained—with a
confidence which no high protectionist has ever
exceeded—that "the prices of articles on our
protected list have increased less than the
prices of articles on our free list." He won
the eminence—good or bad—of being one of the
outstanding targets for shafts of ridicule and

of vexation from our internationalistic free traders.

He undertook to tame the Brazilians who produce coffee, the Mexicans who produce sisal, the Chileans who produce iodine and sodium nitrate, the Frenchmen and Germans who produce potash, the Dutchmen who produce quinine, the Japanese who produce camphor, as well as the British who produce rubber, in their dealings with American consumers.

He fomented a "buyers' strike" in the United States which so reduced our consumption of rubber that the price of rubber broke at one stage from sixty-five cents a pound to thirty-eight.

He outraged much of Wall Street and the whole soul of the *Wall Street Journal* by holding that American bankers should not make loans to "foreign monopolies which control the price of import products to American consumers."

He outraged much of Wall Street again by holding—first among American public men in high office—that the debts of the European Allies to the American Treasury could not possibly be canceled. He said that "these debts were contracted at the urgent request of the borrowers and under their solemn assurance of repayments." He said that "America earn-

estly desires to be helpful to Europe but economic matters require a degree of realism that
will produce justice to the American people as
well as helpfulness to peoples abroad." He
said that "advocating cancellation is only promoting misunderstanding."

He sharpened to a keenness never before
known the advances of American exporters into
markets beyond our boundaries. He did this
not merely by providing them with more foreign information—and better foreign information—through his re-organized Department of
Commerce but also by welding them and the
Department together into a joint public-private,
or private-public, adventuring and merchandis-
ing enterprise.

He brought into existence some sixty or
seventy committees of private business men to
coöperate with the Department. He brought
into existence a large number of "commodity
divisions"—on foodstuffs, on automobiles, on
chemicals, on textiles, and so on—within the Department. He caused the "commodity divisions" and the committees of private business
men to labor concertedly on their specialties.
He gave to our drive for foreign trade the full
force of our public general interest and our
private special interest both.

He caused the editor of the British paper

called the *South American Journal* in London to exclaim:

"It might be well indeed if our authorities would adopt, on behalf of British trade, methods similar to those of the American Bureau of Foreign and Domestic Commerce."

He had rejected international economic alliances at Paris during the Peace Conference. He proceeded now to reject international political alliances also. On the eighth anniversary of the Armistice he could say:

"This day of memories should bring us to a surer resolution that we omit no proper step in statesmanship to eliminate the causes of war in the world; for never again do we wish our sons to leave our shores in our defense. Sure progress in these things requires of us, however, that we should not weaken the strength of our defense or cease to be steadfast in the maintenance of our independence."

One of the most characteristic utterances of Hoover's whole life in summation of his conception of himself was the following:

"I am an individualist. It is not, however, the individualism of other countries for which I would speak. There is a world of difference between Old World individualism and ours.

Our individualism differs from all others.   I am an American individualist.''

But, now, what in the world did he mean by that?   We have touched upon most of the controlling acts of his career.   What have those acts given him, we may ask, of final philosophy, ordered, coherent, focused upon the American future?

CHAPTER FIVE

POLITICAL PHILOSOPHER

HOOVER begins with a mysticism which he considers essential to national bread-and-butter.

He has remarked:

"If you could take away from our people their mystical confidence that one boy's soul is the equal in rights of any other boy's soul, our unique economic success would come clattering down upon our heads in a generation."

The existence of a soul in man and the existence thereupon of inalienable rights constitute for Hoover the beginning of all political thinking. He perceives some such rights—as, for instance, that of free speech—shielded to some extent by the Constitution. His reverence for them, however, goes back of the Constitution. Hoover is an old-fashioned believer in "natural" rights. He conceives that certain rights exist—or should exist—unalterably—if man is to live in full harmony with his nature and his God.

He is accordingly barred at the outset from conceiving himself to be a super-man entitled to subordinate the rights of others to some alleged "higher good" or "national destiny" imagined and decreed by himself. He is also barred from all admiration for schemes whereby society is to be ruled only by "the efficient."

Who are "the efficient"? What board, what bureau, shall certify "the efficient" to the commissioners of elections and thus eliminate "the inefficient" from the polling-lists? Hoover's engineering mind cannot solve that problem. His engineering mind has no improvements whatsoever to suggest upon an equal access by all to a voice in government. He is a democrat because he sees no alternative to democracy except through bureaucratic arbitrary violation of rights; and he regards those rights as originating indefeasibly in the world of the spirit.

He sometimes speaks to this point. He is oftener heard declaring, with an exuberance of enthusiasm almost beyond belief, that:

"In five years we have increased the number of electric washing-machines in our homes from 1,000,000 to 4,000,000."

Anybody who will trail Hoover from mysticism to washing-machines will have the clew both to his character and to his philosophy.

His mind turns every theoretical principle into an instant application. The principle becomes overlaid at once with practice. It becomes a silent assumption. If Hoover went no

farther than the principle, and if he thus could
give more time to it, he could give it more eloquence. He will never be an eloquent man precisely because principles do not remain in his
mind as objects in and of themselves. He trans-
lates them without pause into actions, and then
he speaks of the actions, and they are necessarily relatively earthy and dull.

His principles have to be dragged out of him
by finding him in a moment of leisure—or, let
us say, of respite—and by forcing him to go
back into his mind to regain consciousness of
the reasons why he does what he does.

On one such occasion I questioned him about
certain allusions of his in the newspapers to
"equality" and about certain other allusions of
his to "leadership." These questionings led on
to a discussion of education. What Hoover said
that evening was—as it were—an "introduc-
tion" to the book of his acts. I shall therefore
quote its main points in—so far as I can do so—
his own words.

He said:

"You remark that a lot of very clever people
call democracy a failure. What do they mean
by democracy? They can mean, in practice,
only one thing. Democracy is a system under
which there is all possible equality of opportunity—educational and economic and political.

"The question then is: Who are the people who are to be excluded from equality of opportunity?

"The customary answer is: The ignorant.

"That means, in practice, again, only one thing. It means those who work with their hands.

"Now! Out of some little experience in private life and in public life I will give you an estimate. I will say:

"Take the twenty thousand men who might perhaps be regarded as constituting in this country our creative leadership—our leadership that makes for progress in business, in education, in government. What will you find? You will find, I am confident, that ninety per cent. of them have worked with their hands or come from fathers and mothers who worked with their hands.

"In other words, our revisers of democracy, in search of leadership, would exclude from equality of opportunity precisely the group from which we get most of our leaders.

"I see no sense in that.

"You remark further, however, that a lot of very clever people object to our American mass-education because they think it produces a uniform and monotonous country.

"Where could they have looked? Did they

look at Vermont and then look at Texas? Did they look at our terrific spending and wasting and then look at our terrific saving and home-building? Did they look at our biggest audiences in the world for cheap entertainments and then look at our biggest audiences in the world for the world's best music? Did they look at the cotton-planter in the South and then look at the metal-miner in the West?

"Apparently not. I really must say that it seems to me that our foreign visitors who find monotony here must bring it with them. This country is so various in its activities and achievements that our friends from abroad would be better advised if they would call it the most bewildering social kaleidoscope that ever existed.

"But what makes that variety?

"There indeed we come to the real question.

"I say that what makes our exceptional variety is our exceptional equality of opportunity.

"It is provably preposterous to say that equality of opportunity means a dead level. It means precisely the reverse.

"Human beings are all different. They have different temperaments. They have different talents. In a word, they are various. They are so by nature.

"Give them all then an equal chance, and what happens? Why, the variety in them at once emerges and grows—and grows.

"Equality of opportunity does not suppress the differences between people. It releases them. It accentuates them.

"Out of equality of opportunity, instead of getting anything like a level, we get upheavals, depressions, valleys, hills, abysses, mountains.

"When you say identical chances, you are also necessarily saying differentiated results.

"And it is those results that bring us leadership.

"People think up strange and intricate devices which they claim would produce leadership.

"I think they could spare themselves the trouble. Equality of opportunity produces leadership automatically. It discovers it, develops it, rewards it, exalts it.

"In Europe there is no lack whatsoever in business of what you might call trained private industrial soldiers. Nor is there any lack there of trained technical industrial sub-officers. The lack in European business (compared with American business) is a lack of ambitious and abounding material for industrial colonels and generals and field marshals.

"We have that material here. It is so ambitious and so abounding that it creates new industries for us beside the old ones and on top of the old ones so fast that our established fortunes and our established families are forever passing almost immediately from fore-front to back-ground.

"This material among us is also so vital and so vigorous that it has created for us a unique set of governmental institutions for the preserving of its rights.

"What is the Interstate Commerce Commission? What is the Federal Trade Commission? What are most of our so-called 'regulatory' bodies?

"When you analyze them clear through, you will perceive that their central purpose is to try to preserve equal rights and equal opportunities among shippers, among traders, among investors, among competitors in general.

"We 'regulate' in this country not in order to coerce the individual but in order to make him more free.

"If we go beyond that line, we cease to be ourselves, we cease to be American.

"With us a government can be, and should be, not a mere controlling agency but also a liberating agency.

"That duty of liberation begins at the very moment of the citizen's birth. From that very moment it is the duty of the state to see to it that the chance of every child in relation to every other child is a reasonably decently fair chance.

"Hence the first and foundational duty of the state is the fostering of schools.

"Education is America's biggest business and its best business.

"What is our most spectacular instance of American mass-production? It is not automobiles. It is not steel ingots. It is this:

"We have to-day in institutions of higher learning in this one country more students than exist in such institutions among all the other billion and a half of people in the whole of the rest of the world.

"That mass-production is a mass-production of leadership.

"The state cannot go too far in stimulating equality of educational opportunity. One of the strongest arguments for federal economy is that it leaves more money to states and cities and towns for local schools.

"The state cannot go too far in stimulating equality of political opportunity. It is justified, amply justified, in checking unfair practices of voter against voter or of candidate against candidate and in providing for all voters and for all candidates a fair free field.

"And, finally, the state cannot easily go too far in stimulating actual and genuine and bona fide equality of economic opportunity. It does not provide this equality when it takes an industry over into its own hands for operation. It may then provide equality of salary. It may provide equality of service. It does not in such circumstances provide equality of opportunity. It does not provide American equality—which is equal rights to unequal results.

"Let other nations teach us equality in slavery. They will teach us in vain. Our equality is an equality in freedom.

"What is the duty then, in sum, of the state to that freedom?

"It is more than the duty of a policeman. It is more than the duty of keeping order. It is a duty of promotion. It is a duty of stimulation. If I were to give a phrase to it, I suppose that I might say that I believe in the Individualizing State, the State that can and does make the individual citizen more and more individual.

"That's the individualism—I think—that distinguishes us both from the countries where the government does (so to speak) everything and from the countries where the government does (so to speak) nothing. That's the individualism—I think—that is our individualism, American individualism."

On that confession of faith I felt—and feel—that there are two observations to be made.

In the first place, Hoover's philosophy is very manifestly associated with his own tenacity toward his own experiences. He strove up. He sees life as a striving. He wants to keep it a striving. With all of his traveling, with all of his variety of efforts and achievements, he is a man of a most astonishing continuity of impressions and of ideals.

When he was a boy, the town of West Branch, Iowa, looked big to him. Well, it still looks big.

He once said in a speech to the Iowa Society at Washington:

"Some one may say that my recollections of Iowa are only the illusions of forty years afterwards, but I know better. I have been back and checked up. I was told that everything would have shrunk up and become small and ordinary. For instance, there was Cook's Hill. It was a great long hill where, on winter nights, we slid down at terrific speeds with our tummies tight to home-made sleds. Well, I've seen it several times since. It's a good hill."

That "it's a good hill" was profoundly characteristic and revealing. Hoover never lets go of a scene, of a thought, of an association, once really intimately his.

Stanford was his college. Very well. It is

of Stanford that he has become a trustee. It is
at Stanford that he has fixed his residence. It
is to Stanford that he has given his overpower-
ingly voluminous and inestimably valuable col-
lection of documents bearing upon the Great
War.

He became an engineer. Very well. He since
then has been business man and public man for
many and many a year. He still nevertheless
with the utmost conviction thinks of himself as
a going member of the engineering fraternity.

He fed Belgium. Very well. He cannot for-
get Belgium. He still has the Commission for
the Relief of Belgium Educational Foundation.
It provides endowments to Belgian universities.
It provides scholarships to Belgian boys and
girls desiring higher education. It brings Belgian students and Belgian professors to this
country. It sends American students and
American professors to Belgium. Hoover was
once a factor in Belgian life. That was enough.
He still is.

He once had, in Europe, the American Relief
Administration. He has it in Europe no longer.
But has it really ceased? Not at all. The
moneys left over from it were put into the
American Child Health Association, which lives
and very actively moves in the United States
and has for its object the perhaps distant ideal

that all American children "shall have a healthy childhood and shall reach maturity in the happiness that comes in its fullness only to those whose physical heritage has been safeguarded."

It is this continuity of Hoover's that ties him to the soil, the American soil.

If foreigners have found him too nationalistic in the forwarding of our economic interests abroad and at home, they are only finding that with him Mandalay and Cape Town could never eradicate West Branch.

He is a man indissolubly of his origins.

He spoke once of the economic life of West Branch. It was in the midst of speaking to the Iowa Society of Washington about the rabbits of West Branch and about the angleworms and one-cent hooks and butcher-string fishing-lines of West Branch, and also about the agates which were to be found on the Burlington track and which had the fortunate merit of shining best when you licked them with your tongue before each exhibit. Passing from those lighter recollections, Hoover said:

"Those were days of chores and labor. I am no supporter of factory labor for children but I have never joined with those who clamor against proper work for children on farms outside their school-hours. I speak from the com-

mon experience of most Iowa children of my
day in planting corn, hoeing gardens, learning
to milk, sawing wood, and the other proper and
normal occupations for boys. We had no need
of Montessori schools to teach us application.
Of even more purpose, I can speak of the strong
and healthy bodies that came from it all.

"Yet the Iowa of those days was not without
its tragedies. The medical science of the times
was powerless against the contagious diseases
which swept the countryside. My own parents
were among the victims.

"There was an entirely different economic
setting of farm life in Iowa in those days. I
have a vivid recollection that the major purpose
of a farm then was to produce a living right on
the spot for the family. I know by experience
that a family then produced all of its own
vegetables, carried its grain to the nearest mill
for grinding on toll, cut and handled its own
fuel from the wonderful woods ten miles away
and incidentally gathered walnuts. The family
wove its own carpets and some of its clothes,
made its own soap, preserved its own meat and
fruit and vegetables, got its sweetness from
sorghum and honey. These families consumed
perhaps eighty per cent. of the product of their
land. Twenty per cent. of it was exchanged for
the few outside essentials and to pay interest on

the mortgage. When prices rose and fell on the Chicago market, they only affected twenty per cent. of the product of the farm.

"Now I am not going to recommend the good old days. The standards of living in food and clothing and shelter were high enough for anybody's health and comfort. There was little left, however, for the other purposes of living.

"To-day, with improved opportunities, there are increased difficulties. You know, and I know, that to-day, as the result of the revolution brought about by machinery and by improved methods of planting and reaping crops and of breeding animals, eighty per cent. of the products of the farm must go to market in comparison with the twenty per cent. that used to go. So now, therefore, when the price of agricultural products wabbles in Chicago, it has four times the effect on that family on the farm that it had in the old days. If prices are high, they mean comfort. If prices are low, they now mean real privation for the farmer. This new situation requires new thought and new effort at remedy."

Hoover's devotion to individualism—as expressed in what I have called his confession of faith—goes back to his uncle's West Branch farm. His supplement to individualism—of which I shall now speak—in the course of a

second comment upon that confession of faith—
goes back to the changed social conditions which
he has observed on the West Branch scene as
well as on all the other economic scenes of the
United States.

Hoover, besides being a great private individualist, is a great private collectivist.

He believes most intensely in private voluntary association among individuals for economic
purposes. He believes in them in the field of
agriculture, in the field of business, in the field
of labor.

He has said:

"If we can keep our economic system in so
healthy a state that there is a job for every man,
I for one am willing to trust the organized
American workers to take care of their wages."

He has said:

"Labor, through organization and collective
bargaining, has steadily advanced its interests.
These are, and should be, the bulwarks of
labor."

He has said:

"It is my opinion that our nation is very fortunate in having the American Federation of
Labor."

On the point of trade associations among
business men he has been equally emphatic.

He has said:

"We are passing from a period of excessively individualistic action into a period of associational activities in business. . . . I think we are in the presence of a new era in the organization of industry and commerce pregnant with infinite possibilities of moral progress. . . . We have perhaps twenty-five thousand associational activities in the American economic field. The membership of the associations conducting these activities must be open to all participants in the industry or trade, or else rival organizations come into existence at once. . . . The total interdependence of all industries compels trade associations in the long run to go parallel to the general economic good. . . . I believe that through these forces we are slowly moving toward some sort of industrial democracy. . . . With these private collective agencies used as the machinery for the elimination of abuses and the cultivation of high standards, I am convinced that we shall have entered a great new era of self-governing industry."

On the subject of coöperative societies in agriculture he has gone even farther.

He has said:

"We must develop a unity of control in the shipping of our several agricultural commodities. This is a step beyond the usual conception of coöperative marketing organizations. Agricultural coöperatives have hitherto been most largely concerned in the elimination of unnecessary links in the distribution chain. They should be increasingly concerned in the actual regulation of the flow of their products to market. They should be represented in terminal markets in direct contact with city distributors. . . . These suggestions may be assailed with the charge that they would result in unbearable monopolies controlling prices. In agricultural products, however, there is a self-governing control of prices which distinguishes them from all others. In all agricultural products an excessive price at once starts an overproduction which breaks the price. There can never be a combination of farmers that can for any length of time rob the public. We must maintain laws in restraint of trade against all other characters of commodities. For agricultural commodities we can take those laws off."

It is perfectly apparent, accordingly, that Hoover's individualism is not one that requires every individual to spend all his time fighting every other individual. It is an individualism, on the contrary, which he himself has sometimes described thoroughly accurately as "associational."

I have quoted his strong assertion of the duty

of the state to stimulate individual equality of opportunity—to stimulate what might be called individual individualism. I have now to add that he has been equally zealous in believing that the state should stimulate associational individualism, and in acting upon the belief.

Here we arrive at—or revert to—Hoover's central and genuinely original contribution to our American political science in practice.

Hoover would not merely permit trade associations to exist. He would encourage them to exist as agencies through which the individual can better serve both himself and the State.

I have already illustrated this principle of his in the course of recounting his dealings with the lumber industry. He found in that industry many trade associations. He successfully encouraged them to come together in their "General Lumber Conferences" and in their "Central Committee on Lumber Standards." He successfully stimulated them into forming what might be called a "super-trade-association"; and he made it possible for this "super-trade-association" to accomplish simultaneously the great savings which I have mentioned to individual lumbermen and the great services which I have also mentioned to the country—and to the Government.

This was done—it is to be noted—by governmental initiative. Hoover—for the stimulating of the vitality of private institutions and of private energies—does not at all flinch from that initiative.

It is thus that he is most sharply to be distinguished from those individualists who find their individualism exhausted when, for instance, it has simply denounced and decried all new federal legislation whatsoever.

We have heard a great multitude of statesmen say: "No more laws." We have been obliged to note that usually they have barely uttered that commandment against the rising tide of legislation when it has cunningly swept them out to sea in some new undertow of legislative seeming necessity.

Hoover has put the whole situation into a statement constructive as well as analytical by saying: "We are confronted with the daily demand to extend government in order to cure some abuse or to remedy some evil.

"The arm of government is often a poor cure for abuse and a poor remedy for evil, because it becomes so readily a restraint of liberty.

"The safeguard against the invasion of government into the lives and liberties of our people is that we shall find solutions for abuses and evils outside the government."

In other words, the Government may do one of two things.

It may simply wait negatively, expostulating against new legislation, till popular pressure obliges it to legislate.

Or it may act positively and summon private collective bodies into collaboration with it to forestall public action by competent private action.

Hoover chose that latter course—as we have seen—in the lumber industry and in a very great number of other industries. The remedial lumber laws competently enacted and effectively enforced by the ''General Lumber Conferences'' and the ''Central Committee on Lumber Standards'' have their counterparts in those other industries likewise. It is most certainly no exaggeration whatsoever to say that Hoover has prevented more public legislation by promoting more private legislation than any other public man in the history of democratic government. It is what he has added, as a theory and as a practice, to democratic government on the face of this earth. It is his nickel on the collection-plate of time.

He happened, as Secretary of Commerce, to contribute it directly to the development of the social functions of what we call specifically ''trade associations.'' Presumably he could have contributed it to trade-unions also or to agricultural coöperative societies if they had come within his sphere of jurisdiction.

Even as Secretary of Commerce, however, he has occasionally dwelt upon the possibilities of governmental initiative in relation to our agricultural coöperatives and our agriculture in general. He was the first of our public men to suggest a Federal Farm Board. To such a Board he proposed utterly to deny all power to oppress and exploit our farmers by political "price-fixing." He pointed out with unanswerable simplicity the fatal finish to which such "price-fixing" must come. He said:

"For each different agricultural product there are six times as many families consuming it as there are producing it. Therefore, sooner or later, the paramount political strength of the six families will overcome the political strength of the one family; and it is the six families that will do the price-fixing, and not the farmer."

Hoover perceived that price-fixing is a noose for the farmer. To his Federal Farm Board he proposed to give duties in the direction not of less freedom for the farmer but of more. He expressed them in general terms by saying:

"Compulsion is an instrument which ends its usefulness in the stopping of wrong-doing. If we are to succeed as a people in agriculture, we must set up an organization so sound and so helpful that the producers will be attracted by voluntary self-interest to join the effort. I think that we must devise machinery for the development of such an organization in which the advantages of membership will be so great that it will speedily acquire and control the preponderating marketing of our several agricultural commodities.''

Again, governmental initiative! Again, private energies stimulated toward larger social actions!

Hoover uses this principle even in his playtime. He can be accused of having done one thing for himself as Secretary of Commerce. He has used the powers of his office—as overlord of the Bureau of Fisheries—to try to diminish the time between bites. He has done it by adding a large number of sports-clubs to the activities and ambitions of the Government of the United States.

For Hoover it is a sublime cause. He once described an obstinate and unreasonable opponent as "an extremist who could never have fished for fun." He not only likes fishing but has convinced himself of its profound tranquilizing and moralizing influence. I think his primary prescription for a soundly ethical country would be a meeting-house with a fishing-hole right back of it. Being himself, however, he could not fish without calculating the time between bites and without devising some social apparatus for making that time shorter.

Almost anybody else would simply have said to the Bureau of Fisheries: "Grow more fish and throw them into more holes and streams."

Hoover calculated, however, the mathematical and financial futility of that course. He calculated that fishermen fishing for sport are now getting in fact an average of only 4.45 fish per annum. He calculated that in order to enjoy a full measure of the spiritual blessings brought by fishing they should catch at least 50 fish per annum. He calculated that at least 10,000,000 men and boys—and women and girls—should fish for sport per annum. He thus arrived at the spiritual and mathematical necessity of an annual national catch of 500,000,000 game-fish.

It was clear to him that Congress would never give the Bureau of Fisheries the money for growing those fish. It was particularly clear to him when he calculated that in order to produce 500,000,000 fish who would live to be caught, he would have to produce 250,000,000,-000 little competitive baby-fish just out of their eggs.

He thereupon did exactly what he might have been expected to do. He summoned in the organized and associated Izaak Waltons of the country, as represented by their sports-clubs. He said to them:

"I cannot afford to build government reservoirs for all those fish. I'll nurse them out. I'll keep them till you can see them. Then you take them. Keep them and feed them in pools in your club-grounds. We'll tell you how. You keep them till they are nicely grown. Then you can have half of them for yourselves to let loose in your own streams. The other half I'll take away from you and throw into streams for the farmer-boy and the city-vacationist who doesn't belong to sports-clubs. So you will be doing a good thing for yourselves, and for everybody else, and for the Government, and there will be less time between bites."

Done! Scores of sports-clubs are now at it. They are private institutions. They are public institutions. They retain their freedom. They work for the nation. They do more good. They enjoy themselves more. It is a little homely epitome of Hoover's total conception of the State and the individual.

Those sports-clubs with their public-private, or private-public, fishes are exactly like the trade associations which provide private advisers and private researchers to Hoover's public Bureau of Standards for the general promotion of scientific discoveries available to all industries and all citizens.

Hoover's Individualizing State, his Stimulative State, through its leadership of organized associations of individuals, confers upon them benefits but elicits from them services.

Mussolini has set up in Europe the "corporative" State. The private associations within it are in the end only its agents.

Hoover has dreamed here what might be called by distinction the "coöperative" State. The private associations within it are not agents to it but contributors.

Mussolini has enshrined the idea of the State issuing absolute orders.

Hoover has raised an opposite altar to the citizen rendering free services.

Mussolini's idea is at bottom absolutely and purely administrative.

Hoover's, by distinction, is profoundly and essentially political.

It exhibits Hoover, this mathematical person, this geological person, this engineering person, this commercial person, this administrative person, this humanitarian person, as at summit a political person.

There is a glory of government, and there is a glory of politics. Government is rule. Politics is the gaining of the consent to that rule.   Government without consent is truly no politics at all.

Aristotle, "father of all them that think," has a passage in his work on "Politics" in which he says:

"Some appear to think that a despotic government is a true political form. . . . Such behavior is irrational. . . . That form of government is best in which every man, whoever he is, can act for the best."

In a democratic society, from that standpoint, a ruler's personal qualities are good only if they are given to making it possible for more and more of his fellow-citizens to "act for the best."

Hoover's personal qualities are not therefore in themselves conclusive in his favor, no matter how robust, no matter how brilliant, they may be.   They may with propriety, nevertheless, be here summarized for review and reflection.

Hoover's personal intellectual qualities are primarily—I should say—the following:

Information, imagination, instancy.

He would indeed be a poor sponge if by this time his incessant diurnal doings and his incessant nocturnal readings had not given him a wide wealth of facts.   They have in truth given it to him with an ampleness that is unsurpassed.

I doubt if anybody who is acquainted with the public men of the world's principal countries would seriously claim that there is anywhere among them a superior to Hoover for mere sheer knowledge.

I mean, of course, public-affairs knowledge. Many a statesman excels Hoover in knowledge of poetry, of music, of pictures, of plays, of birds, and even of fishes in what might be called their purely curious naturalistic aspects having nothing to do with the practical labor of hatching them or the practical sport of catching them.

Hoover has little of that promiscuous universality of gleaming curiosity and interest that made Theodore Roosevelt shine on all facets. Many facets of Hoover shine hardly at all. On the other hand, his specialized facets—cut by his actual working experiences and polished by his ensuing unsleeping studies—shine with a radiance that Roosevelt himself could have envied.

Touch Hoover on any subject on which a public man could ever conceivably be called upon to act—the rye-crop in Russia, the growth of the one-industry town in the United States, the volume of brokers' loans in the New York Federal Reserve District, the distribution of power between the Federal Government's "Departments" and the Federal Government's independent "Commissions," the Senate's rules, the depth of water in American oceanic ports, the circumstances surrounding American loans in Bolivia, the price of wheat-land in Argentina and Saskatchewan and Kansas, the results of the direct primary—and he responds not simply with generalizations but with an outbreak of specific detail evincing (for what they are worth) an indefatigable industry and an almost miraculous memory.

When he appears before a Congressional Committee on behalf of a bill, his off-hand answers to off-hand questions are as exact and specific as his deliberately prepared statements.

In a hearing before the Ways and Means Committee of the House of Representatives just after the war Mr. Copley of Illinois happened to ask him:

"What is Austria exporting?"

Hoover said:

"Fancy leather goods, bead work, a certain amount of magnesite, to a total combined value of about $5,000,000 to other countries in the Western Hemisphere since July."

The wayfaring pioneer in Hoover has carried him into contact throughout the world with almost every public-affairs topic possible. The academic scholar in him has made him on each

topic in succession an "expert." His memory
—unrelaxing, unprovided with exits—turns him
now into being in his own one person a sort of
whole university of "experts."

An evening with him when he is communica-
tive is like taking all the Harvard University
post-graduate economic and political courses
from somebody who, in each case, before giving
his course, had lived it. It is like reading a
Baedeker written by a Marco Polo.

Hoover once regaled a stunned lady at dinner
by telling her the future civilization of the world
as forecast by the proportions of bread and
meat in the diet of the farmers of all countries.

He could be the world's biggest bore, with all
those facts of his, if he had nothing else. Then
comes, however, the play of his imagination,
taking the blocks of facts on the floor and
assembling them into all sorts of projected
castles.

This is Hoover's real play. This is his real
pastime. I have noted that he calls the profession of engineering the profession of "creation." He is forever imagining, forever
"creating," some novelty consonant with reality, some "improvement" built upon the
"data" of the matter in hand.

If the matter is the getting of statistics of
cotton in growth, he can astonish his colleagues

by going altogether outside their calculations
and outside the cotton business to say:

"Who travels roads and sees the crops all the
time? Doctors. They won't need to be paid
for traveling. They do it anyway. Just pay
'em for looking, and there you are!"

He once informed me that one of the best
things about dams and reservoirs and other
forms of river-control was that engineers ultimately, by art, will make water-falls much more
beautiful than those made without designs by
Nature. It had a sound as of blasphemy, I
thought at first, but then I began looking at
water-falls with an eye which was awakened
now to the fact of many a valley really naturally
ugly and to the fancy of that valley really de-
signed into beauty.

Hoover sees everything all the time with an
eye for which nothing is wholly arrived at its
height, nothing is incapable of another push up-
ward, if only the eternal verities under it are
surveyed and obeyed.

He told a Supreme Court Justice once that
the new Supreme Court Building ought to be
put out in Potomac Park all by itself, so that the
Capitol with the legislative branch of our Government in it and the White House with the
executive branch in it and the new Supreme
Court Building with the judicial branch in it

would exhibit to all visitors to Washington the
equilateral triangle of the three separated co-
ordinated equal powers of the American Federal Governmental structure.

He would have made the landscaping of the
National City an eternal symbol of the Constitution.

It is to this phase of his character—the imagi-
native phase—that we owe all of his devices
which I have mentioned for expanding the work
of his Department through the services of un-
paid citizen volunteers. Those bodies of costless recruits are not mere turnings of the wheel
of "efficiency." They are inventions.

Finally, with him, upon the heels of information and of imagination, comes an instancy
which by now must have added the equivalent
of a very large number of years to his working
life.

If a man appears in his office and gives him
an idea that he happens to think is good, he is
likely to have the idea dictated and telephoned
and otherwise put into action before the man
can retrieve his hat and coat and get out of the
building.

Hoover is not oppressed by his work. It
does not stay on his chest. It is off it almost as
soon as it is on it.

It took him only a few days, when he went out

on Mississippi flood-relief, to have a private telephone-circuit rigged up from his railroad car to connect him, on his own signals, with every principal assistant of his throughout the flood-region. He felt that he had to be in touch with each of those assistants on calls not of minutes but of seconds.

It is hard for Hoover in narrating his life to put his decisions into any sort of drama for his auditors. There has been no drama. There has been no pause. There has been no suspense. If Hoover had been Hamlet, Shakespeare would never have had a chance to write "To be or not to be." The uncle—or Hamlet—would have been dead in the first act.

Hoover's "data" are laborious. His decisions are effortless.

Such are his qualities that I have called "intellectual." I come now to what I think it is in him that makes him use those qualities in a way that is directed not toward subjugating his fellows but toward making them more and more free to (as Aristotle expressed it) "act for the best."

A man's character is often largely determined by reactions within him to his own impulses.

Hoover's deepest psychological impulse is undoubtedly one of shyness, of sensitiveness, of ingrowingness.

The reaction from that impulse is a search for society.

The reaction from it, further, is an acute consciousness of the personalities of others.

If you could interview all the hermit-crabs in the world who have crawled into shells in all the seas of the world, you would probably (if you could penetrate their feelings) find them unanimous on the proposition that living creatures should have shells.

It is really not one bit surprising that Hoover, who sometimes behaves as if he could hardly bear to look at you, will remember you from the other side of the world and will stretch out his hand to give you a push by wire into something for your advantage.

His whole life, if we brush his intellectual qualities and achievements aside for a moment, has been ingrowingness for himself reacting into tenderness for others.

This is the root of all his "humanitarianism," of his pity toward the weak, toward the suffering, toward children.

It is the root simultaneously of his democracy, of his respect for the individualities of all men and women, of his passion for equality of opportunity for them.

It is the intensity of his own individualism

that makes him so intensely declare and desire theirs.

It is to that end, and by that instinct, that he becomes not himself a colossus but rather an organizer of colossal collaborations.

In the course of these collaborations—so multitudinously personal—he carries, usually, his shell with him. Politics begins indeed to tempt him more out of it. At a dinner addressed by many public men he not long ago made a speech in which, as usual, he told the diners something or other about such things as the average distance to which the lighthouses of the Department of Commerce throw their beams out to sea from Cape Hatteras. At the apparent end of the affair the chairman remarked that it was against the rules of the club to call upon any speaker twice but the speech of the Secretary of Commerce had been so terrible that he would now give him another chance. Ten years ago Hoover would have had to be supported out of the room. Now he rose and in full realization of his committed error reversed it by telling ten minutes of the laughably lighter side of his experiences as an office-holder.

I am not among those who observe only that Hoover may perhaps do politics some good. I observe that most certainly politics has done Hoover a lot of good.

He acts political. He may some day be able to play-act political.

When I say that he acts political, I place him with all those who in the development of our democracy have kept true to its mandate and to its method.

Its method is consent. Its mandate is opportunity.

The ultimate fact about Hoover is that he gives his information, his imagination, his instancy, to following that method and to forwarding that mandate.

Has he a special genius for organization? It is admitted by the whole world.

But what then is his merit?

Say when he is gone that he was a seeker of metals and an organizer of all commodities, of gigantic economic successes, of titanic economic pities, and you will yet have said nothing to recommend him to the abiding recollection of a free people till you have recounted his labors to keep the path of every citizen open wide and wider to more action for himself and to more service to the Republic and till you have then added simply:

"He was an American. He was a Seeker of Consent. He was an Organizer of Opportunity."